STREAMLINED
DECORATIVE SEWING

STREAMLINED DECORATIVE SEWING

RENÉE ROBINSON, *Des*.R.C.A. and

JULIAN ROBINSON, *Des*.R.C.A.

ST. MARTIN'S PRESS
NEW YORK

To

Charlotte, Xavier and Georgina

AFFILIATED PUBLISHERS:
Macmillan & Company, Limited, London
also at Bombay, Calcutta, Madras and Melbourne
The Macmillan Company of Canada, Limited, Toronto.

Contents

About the Authors

Renée and Julian Robinson are fashion designers, authors and lecturers with an international reputation.

Both teach at the Hornsey College of Art, London, where Julian is Director of Fashion Studies. They are also sewing consultants for a national women's magazine and have made many television appearances.

They are both graduates of the Faculty of Fashion Royal College of Art, London.

Introduction

The idea of this book—as with our previous books, *Streamlined Dressmaking, Streamlined Curtains & Covers, and Streamlined Sewing for Fun*—is to make sewing both easy and fun, an exciting challenge rather than an exacting task. It is based on completely new, streamlined methods which have been specially chosen for their simplicity and easy adaptability. It not only shows ways of short-cutting traditional methods, but cuts out the usual inhibiting rules and avoids the complicated mumbo-jumbo of old fashioned craft techniques. The emphasis is on ease and enjoyment which will help even the inexperienced needlewoman achieve instant sewing success.

We will also show you how to prevent your sewing becoming dull or boring, by always being on the look-out for new ideas, as this is part of what makes sewing exciting. Magazines and newspapers provide a fund of new designs and decorative schemes, interesting surface treatments and novel ways of brightening up your sewing. Whenever you see something you like, make a note of it in a scrap-book, adding fabric cuttings, press photographs and articles so that when you are thinking of making something new you can thumb through it to find a wealth of ideas to help crystallize your thoughts, in much the same way as a book of cooking recipes. A scrap-book kept up to date in this way will become as important to your sewing as your scissors or pins.

R. and J. R.

1. Decorative Stitches

In this chapter we are going to explain how to make many decorative stitches in easy-to-learn streamlined methods which short-cut the usual mumbo-jumbo of complicated and old-fashioned needlework techniques. The methods used are slightly unorthodox, and are much frowned upon by the traditional sewing schools, but they are easily understood and will help even the inexperienced needlewoman achieve quick and attractive results.

The variations in decorative sewing are infinite, but we have tried to cover most of the basic principles in this and the following chapters, together with some suggestions of things to make, from cushions and soft toys to dresses and garden hammocks. However, always be on the look-out for new ideas, for novelty is of great importance, and remember to keep your scrap-book up to date with photographs of interesting surface treatments, details from magazine sewing articles, fabric samples and ideas seen on television or in a local shop, etc. When you are thinking of making something new you can turn to your scrap-book to find ideas to help sort out your thoughts.

Finally, for decorative sewing, a small amount of equipment is required: crewel or chenille needles, sharp scissors, a thimble for the middle sewing finger, some sewing cottons or threads, and possibly a free-style embroidery transfer. However, do not overload yourself with too many special gadgets, as these will complicate

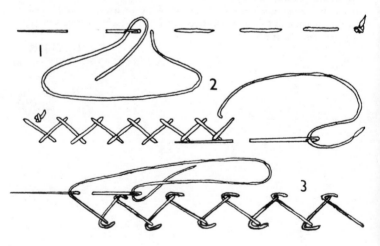

rather than simplify your sewing.

1. **Running Stitch.** This stitch is worked from right to left with the needle passing over and picking up the same amount of material each time, see diagram 1.

2. **Herringbone Stitch** is worked from left to right by taking small stitches alternately above and below each other as shown in diagram 2 opposite.

3. **Coral Stitch** is similar to the herringbone stitch explained above, but is worked from right to left, passing the needle over the thread as shown in diagram 3.

4. **Stem Stitch.** Make regular, slightly slanting stitches along the line of the design, with the thread always emerging on the top left side of the previous stitch as shown above right.

5. **Straight Stitch** can be worked either in a regular pattern to outline a design or can be worked in parallel lines as shown on the right when being used as a filling stitch.

6. **Back Stitch** is worked from right to left with each stitch being made backwards to meet the preceding one as shown in diagram 6 on the right.

7. **Long and Short Stitch** is an irregular form of satin stitch. In the first row the stitches should be alternately long and short, closely following the outline shape. The stitches in the following rows are worked as required to fill the shape effectively as can be seen by diagram 7 on the right.

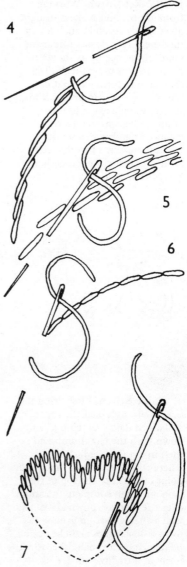

4

5

6

7

9

1. **Blanket Stitch.** Working from left to right make a straight downwards stitch in such a way that the thread passes under the point of the needle as shown in diagram 1 on the right. Pull up the stitch to form a loop and repeat at $\frac{1}{4}''$ to $\frac{3}{8}''$ intervals. This stitch can be used either to outline a design, to attach coloured patches in appliqué work, to neaten a frayable edge, or, if grouped closely together, as a button-hole stitch.

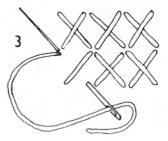

3. **Cross Stitch.** This stitch can be worked en masse by first making a line of diagonal stitches so that the bottom of one stitch is exactly below the top of the previous one, and then working a line of identical diagonal stitches in the opposite direction to complete the crosses as on page 28. Alternatively work the crosses separately as shown on below by making first a left slanting diagonal stitch and then crossing it with a right slanting one, repeating crosses as required.

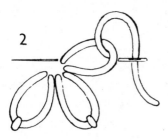

2. **Daisy Stitch.** First bring the needle through near the centre of a planned daisy. Catch a $\frac{1}{2}''$ loop down with the left thumb and then insert the needle next to where it first emerged. Bring the point out next to the top of the loop and then complete the stitch over the loop as shown above. As well as being used in groups to form a flower these stitches can be made next to each other to form an attractive border.

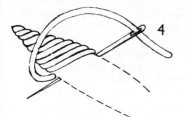

5. Fern Stitch. This simple stitch is just three straight stitches of equal length which radiate from the same point. First bring the needle through on the outline being followed, make a $\frac{1}{2}''$ back stitch, along the outline, bring the needle back through at the first point. Next make a similar stitch diagonally above the first stitch and another one diagonally below the first stitch as shown in diagram 5 below, repeating stitches as required.

4. Satin Stitch. Make diagonal stitches closely together across the shape to be filled as shown in the diagram above, taking care to form a neat, even edge. This stitch can also be used to outline a large shape which can then be filled with other more widely spaced stitches such as the sheaf stitch shown below, cross stitch shown opposite, bead work as on page 34, or couching and ribbon work as on pages 40 and 46, as well as appliqué and patchwork explained in Chapter 3, page 56, etc.

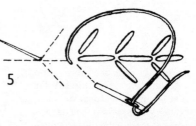

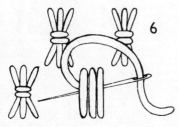

6. Sheaf Stitch is an attractive filling stitch consisting of three vertical satin stitches tied across the centre with two horizontal overcasting stitches. The overcasting stitches are worked round the satin stitches with the needle only entering the fabric to pass on to the next sheaf. The sheaves can be worked in formal rows as shown left or at random spacings and differing angles as a textured filling stitch.

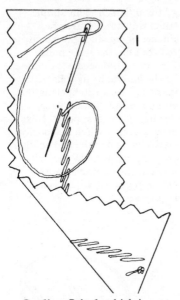

but slightly to its left. Proceed in this way, keeping the stitches fairly evenly spaced.

2. **Chain Stitch** is used for outlining a design where a heavier or more decorative effect is required than can be obtained by using stem or the outline stitch previously explained. It can also be used with rows worked close together as a flower stem as shown on page 67 in combination with appliqué and ribbon work. As with outline stitch many different kinds of thread can be used depending on the effect required, but generally a bold single thread is more effective than a number of loosely twisted strands.

To make the chain first bring

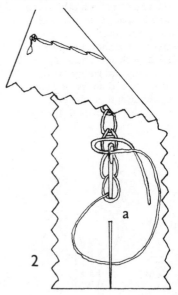

1. **Outline Stitch** which is shown above is used for outlining a design or for any thin solid line that is a main feature, such as flower stems, when it is used in combination with daisy stitch, long and short stitch, rose stitch or similar stitches. This stitch can be made with many different kinds of thread depending on the effect required.

To make the outline stitch point the needle towards you and start stitching from the end of the line nearest to you. Take a stitch $\frac{1}{2}''$ long bringing the needle out halfway along the previous stitch and slightly to its left. Take the next stitch $\frac{1}{4}''$ beyond the first and bringing the needle out level with the end of the first stitch the needle up through the fabric at the end of the line farthest from you, pull the thread towards you and slightly to the left. Hold the thread down with the left thumb and insert the needle just right of where it last emerged. Bring the point of the needle out a short distance away along the line of work. Pull the thread through, keeping the loop of thread under the needle point.

An interesting variation of the chain stitch is the open chain illustrated below. Basically this stitch is made in the same way as the chain stitch explained opposite. The only difference is that instead of bringing the needle straight down the outline being worked the needle is taken diagonally as shown.

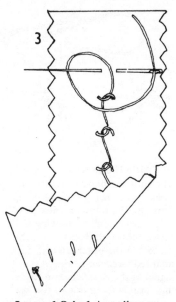

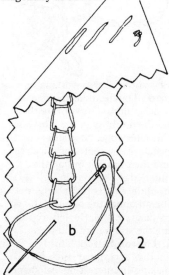

3. **Looped Stitch** is really a loosely looped side stitch and is worked as shown in the diagram above. First bring the thread up through the fabric at the end of the line nearest to you. Lay the thread along the line being worked and hold it down with the left thumb. Take a small stitch under the line and thread, bring the needle up over the loop formed on the left and pull through. Take the thread and again lay it along the line of the design. Hold the thread down with the left thumb and take another small stitch from the right, under the line, and thread about $\frac{1}{2}''$ from the first. bringing the needle up over the loop as shown by diagram 3 above.

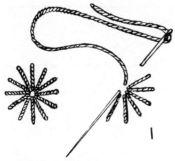

1. **Mille Fleur Stitch** is one of the simplest flower stitches to make. First bring the needle up through the fabric in the centre of a marked circle, drawing the thread through. Next insert the needle at the outer edge of the marked circle and bring it out again at the centre next to the first stitch. Continue in this way as shown above until the flower is complete. This stitch can be worked in many colours and differing textures of thread depending on the effect required.

2. **Rose Stitch.** To make the compact rambler rose stitch shown right, first make several small satin stitches in a bright

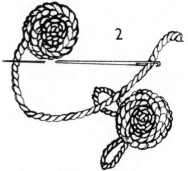

yellow thread. Next work spirally around the rose's centre with a scarlet outline stitch, working from left to right, and letting the needle come out on top of the thread, varying the length of the stitch so that they overlap each other attractively. When making bunches of Rambler Roses change the centre stitch occasionally to bullion stitch or french knots, also changing the colour combinations and thread textures.

3. **Lazy Daisy Stitch** is another

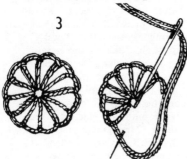

easy stitch. Again working on a marked circle about the size of a jacket button, first bring the needle up through the fabric on the outer edge. Next insert the needle at the centre of the circle and then bring it out on the outer edge between $\frac{1}{8}''$ to $\frac{1}{4}''$ away from the first stitch, laying the thread under the point as shown by diagram 3 on the left, repeating the stitch until complete.

4. **Cretan Stitch.** This is another decorative stitch for making an interesting leaf shape,

or it can be used as a textured filling stitch, stemming stitch, etc. First mark out the leaf or shape required. Bring the needle through centrally at right-hand side, taking a small stitch on lower line, needle pointing inwards and with the thread under the needle point as shown in A. Take a stitch on the upper line, thread under the needle as shown in B. Continue alternately top and bottom in this way until the shape is filled.

5. **Bullion Stitch** is used for embroidering small roses, daisies

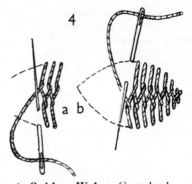

and tulips, or as textured centres to larger flowers. As shown above bring the needle and thread up through the fabric and then make a simple back stitch ¼″ to ½″ long, bringing the needle point out at the starting point, but do not draw the needle through. Next twist the thread around the point of the needle many times and then pull the remaining thread through. Complete the stitch by inserting the needle at the right hand end and draw the thread tight.

6. **Spiders Web** or Cartwheel Stitch is again worked within a marked circle. First make an uneven number of straight stitches as in Mille Fleur stitch shown opposite—five, seven or nine can be used—to form the 'spokes' which are the foundation of the web. Next weave under and over the spokes until the circle is completely filled, or weave only halfway if you prefer the spiky appearance of an unfinished web. This can also be used as a flower stitch if a contrasting coloured centre is worked.

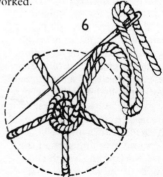

1. **Open Cretan Stitch** is worked between two parallel lines. First bring the thread through on the bottom line at the left side. Insert the needle point, towards you, into the top line ¼″ to the right of the first stitch with the thread below the needle, as shown, and draw through. With the needle facing away from you make a stitch on the bottom line ¼″ to the right of the previous stitch, with the thread under the point of the needle, and draw through. Repeat top and bottom at regular intervals.

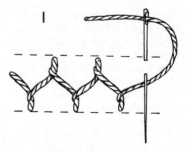

2. **Rambler Rose Stitch** is used to make a larger version of the rose shown on page 14. As a centre make several bullion stitches as described on page 15, using a yellow medium weight thread. Then, using a medium or heavy weight scarlet thread, or several strands of softer thread, work spirally around the centre with longish back stitches, letting the needle come out above the thread as shown above.
Continue working around the rose, varying the length and angles of the stitches so that they overlap attractively.

3. **Vandyke Stitch** is worked between two upright lines ½″ to ¾″ apart. Bring the thread through at A which is just below the top end of the left guide line. Take a small horizontal stitch in the middle of the guide lines ¼″ above A. Insert the needle at B which is opposite A, bringing the needle through ⅛″ below A. Without piercing the fabric, pass the needle under the centre crossed threads as shown below and insert ⅛″ below B. Do not pull the stitch too tightly as this will make an irregular plait. Repeat as shown.

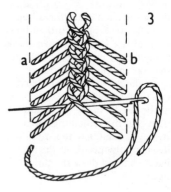

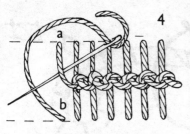

4. **Loop Ladder Stitch.** Make two parallel lines ½″ to ¾″ apart. Bring the needle through in the middle of the lines at the right-hand side of the work. Insert the needle at A on the top line, bringing it through at B, which is immediately below A but on the bottom line. With the thread to the left and under the point of the needle, pass the needle under the centre of the first stitch without piercing the fabric. Insert the needle ⅛″ to the left of A, bringing it through ⅛″ to the left of B and again pass the needle under as shown above.

5. **Scroll Stitch.** This stitch is worked from left to right around a design as an outline, or border stitch. The working thread is looped to the right and then back to the left on the fabric as shown below. Inside this loop the needle takes a small slanting stitch to the left on the line of the design, with the thread of the loop under the point of the needle, the thread is then pulled through. Space the stitches evenly and do not pull the thread too tightly as this makes irregular scrolls.

6. **Fishbone Stitch** is used for filling small shapes such as leaves or petals. Bring the needle through at the left-hand point of the shape and make a small straight stitch along the centre.

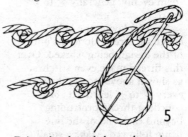

Bring the thread through again at the point just above the first one and make a sloping stitch across the base of the first stitch. Bring the thread through just below the starting point and make a similar sloping stitch to overlap the previous stitch. Continue working alternately on each side until the shape is filled.

Couching consists of a bold thread or thin braid applied on to the fabric surface by means of small stitches of fine thread, as a heavy outline, or when an intertwining pattern is required.

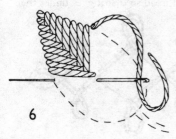

17

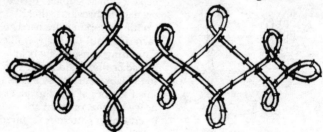

In applying the heavy thread or braid the stitches are usually planned to show and may even be of a contrasting colour, so care should be taken to space them evenly, generally $\frac{1}{2}''$ to $\frac{3}{4}''$ apart.

Start by laying the bold couching thread along the outline of the design being worked. Over this thread make even stitches, as shown above, across the thread every $\frac{1}{2}''$ to $\frac{3}{4}''$ leaving $1''$ of couching thread protruding beyond each end of the line being followed. Make a small hole in the material with the aid of a stiletto at each end of the design and draw the heavy thread through with a crochet hook, securing the ends with a few extra stitches.

Interlacing is the intertwining of coloured threads, ribbons or braidings into evenly made decorative stitches or novelty woven fabrics. As can be seen by the illustration opposite, the interlacing need not be very complicated, though the one shown bottom right requires a little more thought. To make the simple interlaced band first make two parallel lines of machine stitching, or hand back-stitching if preferred, $\frac{1}{2}''$ to $\frac{3}{4}''$ apart. Working from left to right bring a matching or contrasting coloured thread through on the lower left hand corner. Following diagram 2 make a stitch through the top line of threads $\frac{1}{4}''$ to the right of the first stitch, laying the thread so that it goes under the

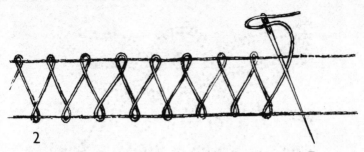

2

needle as shown, also passing the needle through the lower line to make a stitch ½″ away from the first stitch. The next stitch is made with the point of the needle facing away from you, again laying the thread so that it goes under the needle. Make the third stitch through the top line ½″ away from the previous loop and the fourth one ½″ away from the bottom one, repeating top and bottom until complete.

The foundation of the interlaced border shown below is a double row of herringbone stitches worked in two journeys, with the stitches being intertwined to make a framework for slotting through the interlace

heavier thread or cord. Do not pull the foundation stitches tightly as the interlacing thread tends to draw them together. When both rows of herringbone stitch are worked, bring the interlacing thread through in the middle of the foundation stitches on the left hand side. Following the diagram closely intertwine the interlacing thread from the centre to top crossings until the end of the row is reached. Lace the thread round the last centre cross and then work back in a similar fashion along the lower half of the foundation. The last two crosses on the diagram have been left unlaced so that the construction may be seen clearly.

3

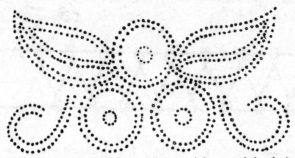

Italian Quilting is just one of the many other ways of enriching the surface of a fabric. It consists of making two parallel lines of stitches $\frac{1}{8}''$ to $\frac{1}{4}''$ apart through two layers of fabric and then slotting thick wool between the layers, to raise the design.

1. Mark the chosen design on to a soft piece of backing fabric which is not too closely woven—cheesecloth is ideal—and then tack the marked material on to the wrong side of the top fabric.

2. Make small running stitches just less than $\frac{1}{8}''$ away from the outline of the design and a second row a scant $\frac{1}{4}''$ inside the design, so that there are two parallel stitch lines just under a

$\frac{1}{4}''$ apart right round the design.

3. For the padding thread a blunt-pointed large-eyed tapestry needle with thick soft knitting wool, matching colour if possible, or a bright contrasting colour if a shadow effect is required. Slot the needle between the stitched layer, making long stitches where possible, but bringing the needle out when a curve prevents going any further. Insert the needle again in the same place and proceed as before, leaving small loops between the stitches so that the padding is not drawn too tightly. Do not use knots, simply clip away any unwanted ends after completing the padding.

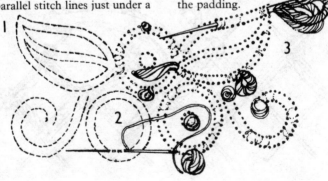

Decorative Hems. There are many decorative ways of stitching hems. Just a few are shown on the right, whilst many more ways of decorating hems are shown throughout this book.

1. **Buttonhole Stitch** which is grouped in threes or fours as in diagram 1 makes an interesting finish on the raw edge of a firm non-fraying material, or over a folded edge if required. The stitch illustrated is single purl buttonhole stitch with a blanket stitch every fifth stitch. Starting on the left insert the needle from behind $\frac{1}{4}''$ in from the folded edge. Make a second stitch close to the first, laying the thread so that the point goes over it, and then draw it up to form a loop. Make a third and then a fourth stitch in the same way. The fifth stitch is made $\frac{1}{4}''$ to $\frac{1}{2}''$ away from the first group and becomes the first stitch of the next group, repeating until finished.

2. **Scalloping.** First mark out the edge to be scalloped and fill with long and short padding stitches as shown on page 9. Work over the padding stitches with single purl buttonhole stitches as in diagram 2, inserting the needle on the upper outline and bringing it out on the lower one with the needle over the thread, keeping the stitches evenly spaced. When all of the scallops are complete, trim away the surplus fabric, taking care not to clip any of the stitches, removing all the surplus fabric to avoid a ragged appearance.

Insertion Stitches. The general principle behind these stitches is the joining together of two pieces of fabric, which can be either cut or turned edge.

1. **Zig-Zag Stitch,** which is shown on the right, is the simplest insertion stitch. First take two pieces of fabric of equal length. Turn under $\frac{1}{2}''$ along the edges to be joined and press these flat. Butt these edges together. Bring the needle and thread out of the top right-hand strip $\frac{1}{8}''$ away from the folded edge. Slip the needle underneath the left-hand folded edge and bring out the needle $\frac{1}{8}''$ in from the fold and $\frac{1}{8}''$ below the first stitch, as in diagram A. The second stitch is made by slipping the needle under the right-hand edge and bringing it out $\frac{1}{8}''$ away from the folded edge and $\frac{1}{4}''$ away from where the first stitch started. Continue stitching left and right until the seam is completed.

Faggoting. This is a much neglected yet extremely decorative method of joining two pieces of fabric together. It differs slightly from the insertion stitch explained above in that the folded edges to be joined are first tacked on to a strip of stiffish paper the required distance apart, generally between $\frac{1}{4}''$ to $\frac{1}{2}''$.

2. **Criss-Cross** faggoting stitch is shown in diagram 2 on the right. Start by bringing the needle and thread out on the right-hand side bottom edge $\frac{1}{8}''$ away from

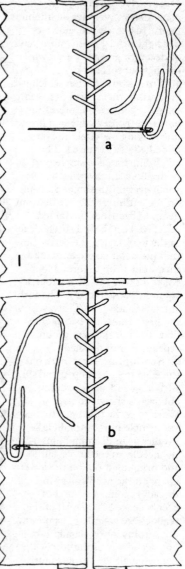

a

1

b

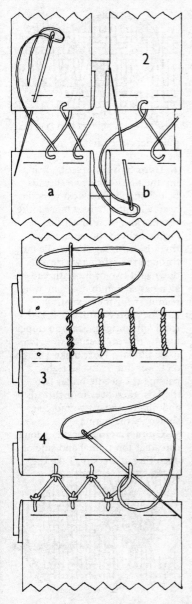

the fold. The next stitch is made on the top folded edge $\frac{1}{4}''$ to the left of the first stitch and passing the needle over the thread, as shown A. The third stitch is made on the bottom edge $\frac{1}{2}''$ away from the first, again taking $\frac{1}{8}''$ stitch, as shown B, passing the needle over the thread. Continue stitching top and bottom until complete.

3. **Bar Stitch.** Take a small stitch on the lower right-hand side of the prepared fabric pieces. Take a stitch on the upper edge directly opposite. Twist the thread around the point of the needle several times, as when making a bullion stitch, before taking a stitch directly over the first. Pull the thread to form a bar, but not so tightly as to distort the spacing. Slip the needle between the fabric layers for $\frac{1}{2}''$ and make another bar stitch, continuing at $\frac{1}{2}''$ intervals until complete.

4. **Knotted Stitch.** Start on the bottom left-hand side of the prepared fabric pieces with a small stitch $\frac{1}{8}''$ away from the folded edge. Make a similar stitch on the top edge $\frac{1}{4}''$ towards the right. Pass the needle behind the thread as shown by diagram 4 to form a loop, with the needle sloping from left to right, making a knotted stitch over the thread. Make another stitch on the bottom edge $\frac{1}{2}''$ from the first and make a similar knotted stitch. Continue working top and bottom until completed.

Drawn Threadwork as its name implies is carried out by withdrawing threads from an evenly woven fabric and then decorating over the spaces left with embroidery stitches. Various decorative stitches or ribbons can also be intertwined with the the warp or weft threads or complete motifs such as spiders web filling can be used on open corners, as can the Hardanger stitches shown on page 28, etc.

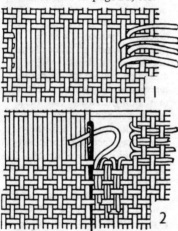

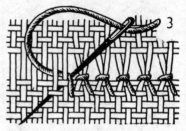

1. Withdrawing Threads. First cut across the required number of threads and withdraw these carefully as shown in diagram 1 above, leaving sufficient threads at ends to darn away invisibly.

2. Darning Ends. Darn each cut thread separately into the fabric over and under each woven thread, as shown in diagram 2 above, taking care to

pull each stitch neatly into position.

3. Hem Stitch. Start by bringing the needle out two threads below open work. Next pass the needle behind two or more loose threads and then insert the needle behind the same loose threads, bringing the needle out through the fabric two threads down and two or more threads along as shown in diagram 3, in readiness for the next stitch.

4. Chevron Stitch is worked from left to right. Start on upper line by making a stitch over two loose threads. Next make a stitch on lower line ¼″ to the right, passing the needle under two threads, then over four threads and finally under two more as shown by diagram 4.

5. Open-Lacing. Fasten a long thread at top right-hand side of open thread section. Take the

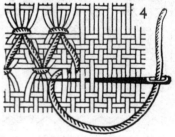

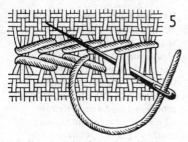

5

needle over six threads and then pass it back under three, emerging above the thread. Make another stitch over six threads and back under three, repeating until top row is completed. Fasten another length of thread to the bottom left-hand side and reverse the stitch, over six back, under three, as above, until open-lacing is finished.

6. **Interlacing.** Interlaced hem stitch is made over groups of open threads which have been hem-stitched to produce an even ladder of loose threads. Fasten a long thread at right-hand side centrally on to the first ladder. Insert the needle from left to right under the second group and twist the needle over so that it is now right to left, bringing the second group over

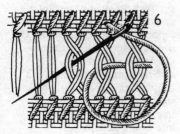

6

the first one as in diagram 6. Pull thread through and repeat as shown below left.

7. **Spiders Web** corner-filling stitch is worked over the open corners left after withdrawing both the warp and weft fabric threads. Working from corner to opposite diagonal corner and centre to centre make an eight armed cross as shown below. Starting with a centre knot weave the thread over and under the alternate arms until a neat coil

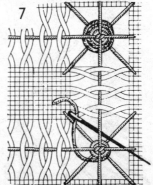

7

is formed, generally three to four times round, finishing with a neat knot at the back.

Decorative Corners. Many other interesting and decorative corner and interlacing stitches can be made in openwork embroidery in addition to those already shown. If you are interested in this type of work many good easy-to-follow pamphlets and patterns are available, published by the Coats Sewing Group, 50 Bothwell Street, Glasgow, C2, Scotland.

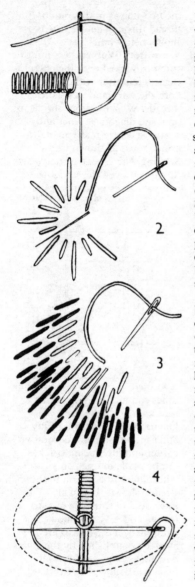

French Cut-work or Richelieu work is a very distinctive form of stitched and cut work which is ideally suited to decorative table linen, window-blind ends, bedspread edges, etc. Basically it consists of cut edge interlinking motifs which have their raw edges covered by buttonhole stitches. The in-between areas are then cut away. Occasionally surface stitchery is added to enhance this cut-work, giving a distinctive decorative richness. Shown here are a few of the basic stitches used, but many others such as those shown on pages 10 and 11, 14 and 15, or elsewhere in this or our other books, can be used with equal success.

1. **Buttonhole Stitch** is the basic stitch used in this form of cut-work. As shown in diagram 1 on the left the stitch is made over the marking line. First bring the needle out just below the design line on the left hand edge of the motif. Insert the needle just above the line, taking a straight downwards stitch with the thread under the needle point to form a loop. Make another stitch above the line a scant $\frac{1}{8}''$ away from the previous one and repeat with the thread under the needle to form a loop again as illustrated top left.

2. **Straight Stitch.** This is a simple single-spaced stitch worked either in a regular or irregular manner to form an interesting pattern.

3. **Long and Short Stitch** is similar to the embroidery stitch shown on page 9, with the stitches being made in varying lengths as shown on the left. This stitch is generally used for filling an area requiring a textured look, and can be worked in several colours for an interesting and varied effect.

with many other decorative sewing techniques which can be found on pages 10 to 17, 32 to 37, 50, etc. can be used to supplement the basic cut-work techniques.

6. **Automatic stitches,** which can be made on most zig-zag swing needle machines, can also be used to great advantage

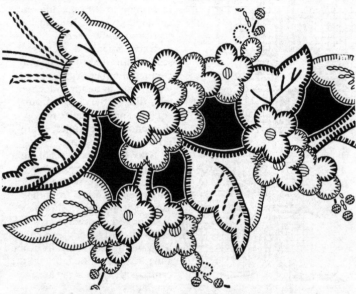

4. **Stitched bars** are also used extensively in French cut-work. The stitch used is the same as explained for buttonhole stitch, the only difference being that it is worked over several looped threads as shown in diagram 4 on the left.

5. **Satin Stitch,** stem stitch, cross stitch, chain stitch and various flower stitches, together

to outline French cut-work instead of using the traditional buttonhole stitch, adding just a few hand finishing stitches to enrich the finished look. Other forms of surface decoration such as slotted ribbon work, appliqué, couching, beading and faggoting can be added, combining several different techniques into a single unified design.

27

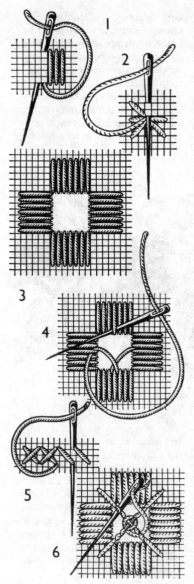

Norwegian threadwork or Hardanger is a form of stylized embroidery and cut-work which is best made on an even weave linen or similarly textured fabric. The stitches are generally easy-to-make interesting blocks of satin stitch, squares of cut-work, and decorative filling stitches, which are at their best if worked in a single colour on a different coloured ground fabric, such as scarlet on holly green.

1. **Satin Stitch.** Work this stitch from right to left over a counted number of threads which vary in depth and length according to the design, from squares and rectangles to diamonds and triangles, or any other geometric shape.

2. **Star Eyelet** consists of eight stitches which are worked over a square of fabric with each stitch being worked from the same central hole, as shown.

3. **Blocked cutaways** are satin-stitched blocks worked horizontally and vertically around a marked area. The fabric in the centre is then cut away as in diagram 3.

4. **Dove's Eye Filling** or similar looped filling stitches are worked over the cut away areas. The one shown in diagram 4 consists of stitching from the centre of each satin-stitched block, looping the thread into an attractive pattern.

5. **Cross Stitch.** Work an even line of diagonal stitches so that the bottom of one stitch is

exactly below the top of the previous one, then reverse the stitch, working more diagonals to complete the crosses. Alternatively work the cross stitch as shown on page 10.

6. **Stitched Fillings** are made diagonally across satin-stitched cut-outs. First work two twisted bars across the space as in diagram 6; the thread is then passed over and under the bars twice, and then under and over.

7. **Overcast Bars** can be worked at the junctions of several interlinking cut away areas or where drawn threadwork—explained on page 24—and Hardanger are used together. To work these overcast bars, first withdraw the number of threads required, as in drawn threadwork, and separate the remaining threads into bars. Overcast these evenly, as illustrated in diagram 7, as many times as required to cover the group of threads completely.

8. **Woven Bars** are a variation on overcast bars and are used in both Hardanger and drawn threadwork. To work woven bars first withdraw an even number of threads from the fabric and separate the remaining loose threads into bars by weaving over and under half the even number of threads as in diagram 8 on the right, until the group of loose threads are completely covered.

Hardanger threadwork can also be combined with drawn thread-

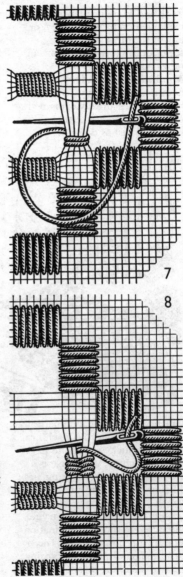

7

8

work and French cut-work as explained on pages 24 to 27, or any of the other decorative techniques shown in this or our other books.

Machine Embroidery. In addition to the many decorative hand stitches already explained there are many more stitches which are just as decorative

sewing machine.

Embroidery Transfers. Many different embroidery designs can be worked out by most experienced needlewomen, while those who are less experienced can buy extremely good transfer designs from most sewing shops. These transfers are ironed on to the fabric as a guide to the stitching

which can be made automatically on most swing-needle machines. If you are lucky enough to have such a machine, whether it is a Bernina, a Neechi, a Viking, an Elna or a Pfaff, it would be well worth your time experimenting with the various stitches, trying out different thread combinations, finding out how to use all the little gadgets and really learning how to make the most of your

details which are fully explained in the instruction leaflet sold with the design. Also explained are the various needles to use and what embroidery threads to buy. But once you have a little experience you can try some experiments, choosing different colour combinations or different thread textures to suit your own decorative ideas.

Traditionally skeins of Anchor

Stranded Cotton, Tapisserie Wool, or Perlita are used, as these can be bought at most shops in a wide range of colours, but it can be great fun to supplement these with knitting wool, raffia, strands of leather and plastic, buttons, russia braid, crochet thread, rug wool, and even coloured string. Just look around and use the most interesting for your decorative sewing.

Decorative things to make can range from toys to party clothes or anything which takes your fancy, so when starting to make something new don't just make the same old things that you have always made, try something different for a change. Remember, always be on the look out for new ideas, as this is what makes sewing fun. Keep a scrap-book for writing down your ideas, or for sticking in various photographs and magazine articles. If you are making or decorating some new sheets spend a little time looking at the latest Swiss embroidered ones in a quality shop. If you are making some dolls or soft toys look through those in a big store to see how they are made and decorated. If you would like to make some decorative cushions or a bed-spread then look at some recent magazines to help you sort out your thoughts. In other words don't just sew for sewing's sake, make it enjoyable and an exciting challenge rather than an exacting task.

31

2. Bead and Ribbon Work

Beads and ribbons are often used as dress trimmings, on cushions or bedspreads, on belts or shoes, for lampshades or blind fringes, either by themselves or combined with embroidery stitches to add a glint and sparkle that embroidery alone does not have. Designs for beading and ribbon work are very similar to those used for embroidery and can be adapted from many of the bolder transfer designs, whilst many other designs can be worked out once you have had a little experience at this kind of decorative sewing.

The following 23 pages are only intended as an introduction to bead and ribbon work, as the other methods of decorative sewing which are explained in the other chapters of this book are intended to be liberally interpreted and combined together to help you develop original ideas of your own. Remember, as there are no inhibiting rules, and as new ideas are continually appearing on the market, it is best to keep an open mind so that you can choose the most exciting designs and trimmings available for your sewing now.

Do remember, however, that the basic idea is to enhance the look of a particular article, making it more interesting or adding a touch of originality, so to obtain the maximum effect your bead and ribbon work should be well made, as irregular sewing will detract from the finished appearance rather than enhancing it.

1. **Single beads** can be sewn on with silk or terylene thread using a thin sewing needle or a special beading needle which is very fine so that it slips through the small openings of fine beads easily. Alternatively a beading hook can be used if a large design is being beaded, but this is a special technique which is best left for those who have a lot of spare time to practice.

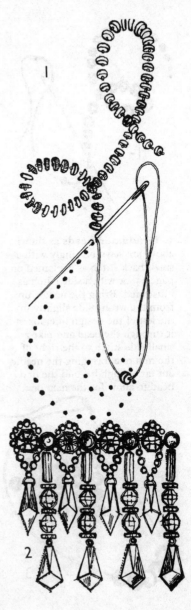

The beading method shown in diagram 1 on the right illustrates how beads are sewn on one at a time along a marked out design line, with the beads being close enough together to avoid a stringy effect. First mark the design on the right side of the material and then bring the needle up from the wrong side at the top right hand side of the line to be followed. Insert the needle through one of the beads and take a small back-stitch in the material as shown, bringing the needle out far enough beyond the first bead to allow for sewing on the next one. Repeat at regular intervals until the design is complete.

2. **Beaded Fringes** can be made by threading several small beads on to a strong silk, linen or terylene thread and then looping back through a larger bead adding crystal drops, metal sections, coloured bugles and novelty beads as required, before once again threading several more small beads and looping back again, repeating until the decorative fringe is completed.

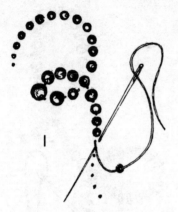

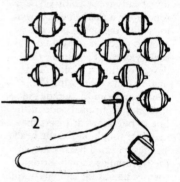

2. **Large beads** can be sewn on with a normal running stitch as shown below, but for safety a small knot or back stitch should be made after attaching several beads in case the thread breaks during wear. First bring the needle out on the right hand side of the design. Insert it through a bead and then make a small forward stitch as illustrated by diagram 2, allowing just enough gap between the stitches to be filled by the bead.

1. **Graduated beads** as shown above are sewn on singly with a small back stitch as explained on page 33, or with a side stitch as illustrated. Bring the needle up from the wrong side slightly to the left of the design line, insert it through the bead and take a small side stitch to the right of the first one, bringing the needle out far enough beyond the first bead to allow for the next one.

3. **Groups of beads,** as shown on the left, can be threaded on to the needle and held with a single stitch. To do this, first bring the needle up through the material at the end of a line and then string on enough beads to fill the space marked. Insert the needle at the other end, as shown, and make a small knot or back stitch to hold securely, adding a stitch across the centre if required. Do not cut the thread between the adjacent lines unnecessarily.

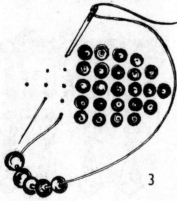

34

4. **Sequins.** Single sequins can be sewn on with the aid of a small coloured bead as shown by the illustration below. Using a very fine needle bring it up through the fabric to the right side. Pass the needle through the centre of a sequin and a bead, and then back through the sequin and fabric to the wrong side. Repeat to complete a pattern, making a back stitch after every tenth sequin to hold securely. To apply sequins in

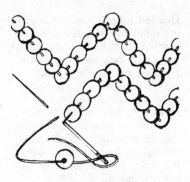

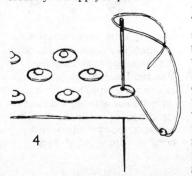

4

various sequin motifs and clusters. To apply the sequin strips simply slip- or run-stitch these along the garment edge, securing the thread with a back stitch every 2″ to 3″. Sequin motifs or clusters should be stab-stitched with each cluster being secured with a knot. If the maker's thread has started to unravel it is wisest not to pull or knot it but simply stick it down with UHU glue or a little nail varnish.

rows first bring the needle up through the material and the centre hole of a sequin and then take a small stitch over the edge. Next bring the needle up again through the fabric, $\frac{1}{8}$″ away from the edge of the first and make a back stitch through the centre of another sequin which has been positioned to cover the previous stitch as illustrated top right. Repeat until all are applied.

5. **Sequin Strips.** Ready-made sequin strips can be bought in many attractive patterns as can

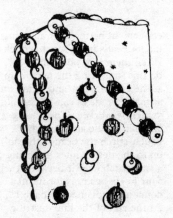

Beaded Edges. Beads or sequins are applied to the edges of a garment in much the same way as previously explained, but as it is generally better to apply this type of decoration to a finished edge, care should be taken to conceal the back of the stitches. This is done by making sure that you never bring the needle right through to the back of the fabric but slip it between the layers to the next stitch.

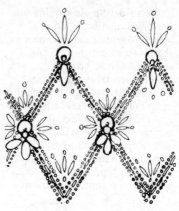

Couched Beading. A very

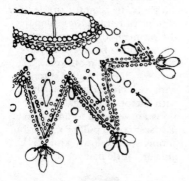

any surplus beads and then pass the thread through to the back of the fabric and fasten securely.

Beaded Lace. Single lace motifs can be sewn on to a net or lace underbodice with the aid of an assortment of beads and sequins as illustrated opposite, with a border of drops being sewn on

convenient method for applying lots of beads in lines is to couch-stitch them into position. To do this first bring the needle up at the end of a line and string on as many beads as can be conveniently worked. Then using another needle and thread, couch-stitch the beaded thread on to the design lines by taking a tiny stitch over it between each four to six beads as for normal couching explained on page 18. At the end of the line unstring

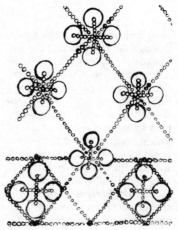

the bottom edge to complete the design.

Beaded Tassels can be made in an unending variety simply by threading a selection of beads on to a strong silk or terylene thread, looping, knotting and firmer to handle and easy to attach.

Loops and Drops can be attached singly or in clusters, threading one on to your needle at a time, or a dozen. There are no rules as long as the finished

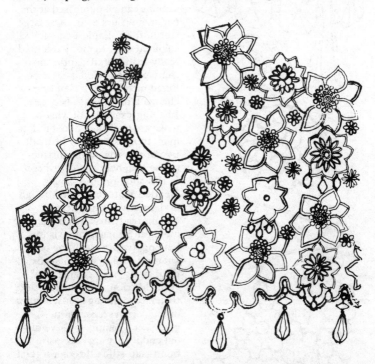

twisting them together as required. They can then be attached directly to an edge or suspended between other beads. Ready-made tassels can be purchased at most large stores. They are usually made on a backing tape which makes them effect is good and the beads do not drop off at the first wearing.

Fashion Fancies. New ideas are continually appearing on the market, so keep an open mind and use the nicest available now, as next year they may no longer be in fashion.

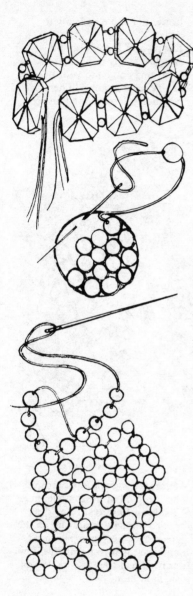

On these two pages are shown just a few of the things which can be made with beads, from bracelets and buttons to lampshades, bags and belts. As explained earlier, a seemingly unending variety of beads and sequins can be purchased at the trimming counters of most large stores, from simple single-holed coloured discs to multi-coloured ready-made motifs, and from shiny plastic to tinted crystal or fluted metal, with lots of ever-changing novelties in between. Just four examples of what to make are explained here but lots more things can easily be made by improvising on the instructions given here and elsewhere in this and our other books.

Beaded Buttons. Many designs of decorative buttons can be bought ready made, and many more can be made by twisting, looping, twirling, plaiting or knotting cord, raffia, rouleaux, dyed string, pipe cleaners, or even electrical wire covering and then incorporating beads, sequins, motifs, dried seeds, plastic pieces, etc. Simply try several out and if they are successful blind-stab-stitch through several times to hold firm and either work a bar across the back to act as a shank or sew on to a covered button as shown.

Decorative Buckles are made by twisting, looping and knotting cord or ribbon around a simple metal buckle and then covering with beads and sequins or in-

numerable other ways to match
buttons or cuff links, or to use
on their own. Try making a
simple one first and then anything
goes.

Bracelets or simple beaded
necklaces can be made by
threading beads on to shirring
elastic or beading thread. The
designs can be as simple as the
bracelet shown top left, or the
threading can be done in a more
complex way as shown bottom
left. This inter-linking of groups
of beads can also be used for
making belts, watch straps,
neckties or even bright shiny
beaded bags.

Beaded Belts can also be made
in many different ways from
plaiting ribbon or knotted string-
work to covering a ready-made
webbing belt with a pattern of
beads and sequins, odd buttons,
brass curtain rings, metal loops
and other decorative oddments
as shown below.

1. Collect together as many
beads, old metal or pearl buttons
as you can find—an assortment
of sizes is best—together with
various rings, loops and other
decorative oddments.

2. Wash these beads, buttons
and loops in mild soapy water,
using a soft scrubbing brush to
get into the corners and grooves,
drying them thoroughly with an
ordinary hairdryer and soft towel
to prevent rust and staining.

3. Arrange them into a pleasing
pattern on to a cheap webbing or
fabric belt, and using silk button-

hole twist or linen thread, stitch each button, bead and loop into position, starting with the largest loops first. These should be sewn on at regular intervals, with the smaller ones being attached in a decorative pattern around them and a few extra novelties scattered in between.

on page 67, or any of the other methods of surface decoration as explained in the other chapters of this book.

When working this type of bold cord decoration, the outline of the design must be couch-stitched first. This consists of applying a coloured cord or bold

Couched Embroidery or couch-stitched cord work is a very decorative bold embroidery which is both simple and quick to do. Thin cord, braid, or special couching threads are used instead of the usual embroidery stitches and these can then be combined with looped ribbon work as shown on page 44, soutache work as on page 88, appliqué work as

thread around the edge of the design and fixing it by means of small stitches of finer thread made across the cord as explained on the opposite page. These stitches are usually planned to show and may even be of a contrasting colour. After stitching the cord around the outline of the design the cord can either be couched in ever-decreasing

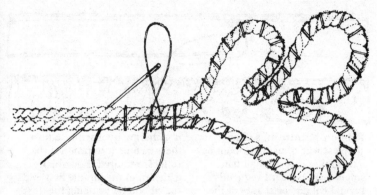

spirals as in the stylized butterfly shown left, or the inner shapes can be filled with loops of ribbon, beads and sequins, or embroidery filling stitches as required.

To apply couch stitched cording first lay the cord or heavy thread on the line to be followed, making regular straight stitches over it as shown above, or with a blanket stitch as shown below. The stitches should be evenly spaced approximately every $\frac{1}{2}''$ to $\frac{3}{4}''$ and made with a matching or contrasting thread as the design requires. Remember to leave $1''$ beyond each end of the line being worked so that the threads can be neatened by drawing them through to the wrong side. Either thread them through with the aid of a large-eyed darning needle or make a hole in the material with the aid of a stiletto, being careful not to break any threads, and then draw the heavy thread through with a small crochet hook, securing them with a few extra stitches. See page 61 for couched appliqué, also page 17.

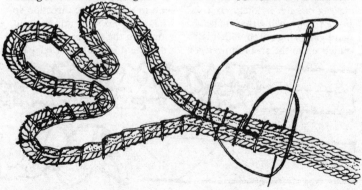

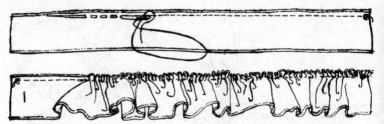

Ribbon Trimmings. The simplest way of using ribbons as a trimming is to apply it flat, singly or in bands. Frequently several colours or shades of the same colour are used with novelty ribbons such as picot-edge, moire and velvet ribbons being interspaced with the plainer grosgrain and satin varieties. The method of applying flat bands of ribbon is first to tack the upper or inner edge of the ribbon into position and then to sew by machine or by hand on the tacked edge leaving the other edge free.

Gathered ribbon. Ribbons can be gathered along one edge as shown above, in the middle as illustrated by diagram 2 or in a zig-zag manner by diagram 3. For a ribbon frill either make a hand gathering stitch which is pulled up to the size required, or if gathering by machine adjust the attachment to produce the fullness required. For ribbon gathered in the middle first fold the ribbon by bringing the selvedges together and creasing to mark the exact centre.

Shell Gathering. A novel effect known as shell trimming is obtained by gathering the ribbon in a zig-zag from edge to edge as in diagram 3. To ensure evenness in the gathering mark the ribbon with zig-zag creases. To do this lay the ribbon right side up and fold the right hand end so that the selvedge is lying straight across the ribbon at right angles to the rest of the ribbon, creasing the fold. Now fold the end in the opposite direction so that a second fold runs at right angles to the first crease and meeting it at the upper edge and

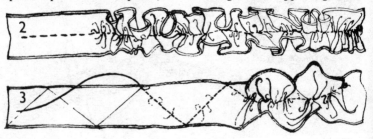

press. Make the third fold like the first, etc., and continue until all the ribbon is marked. Gather along the creases as shown, adjusting the fullness evenly when you draw up the thread.

Ribbon Stitching or slotted ribbon work is another form of bold decorative stitch work which is very easy to do. As in normal embroidery many stitches can be made ranging from the simple ribbon bow stitch, shown on the right, which is ideal for trimming a cot blanket or baby's sleeping bag, to the flower stitches shown on page 46, which would make an attractive centrepiece. As illustrated the stitches are as simple to make as basic embroidery stitches, the only differences are that the needle should have a large eye and the fabric used should be slightly open weave to allow the ribbon to slot in and out easily.

Ribbon Flowers. First mark a circle using a 2/- or 10p piece, then with the aid of a chenille needle, or similar large oval-eyed blunt-pointed needle, and $\frac{1}{2}$ yard of $\frac{1}{4}''$ wide satin ribbon, bring the needle up through the fabric on the edge of the marked circle. Make a $\frac{3}{4}''$ long stitch at the centre of the flower, bringing the needle up on the outer edge $\frac{1}{4}''$ away from the first stitch. Make a second $\frac{3}{4}''$ stitch to the centre, bring the needle up $\frac{1}{4}''$ away from the second stitch as shown on the right, making regular stitches at $\frac{1}{4}''$ intervals right round the

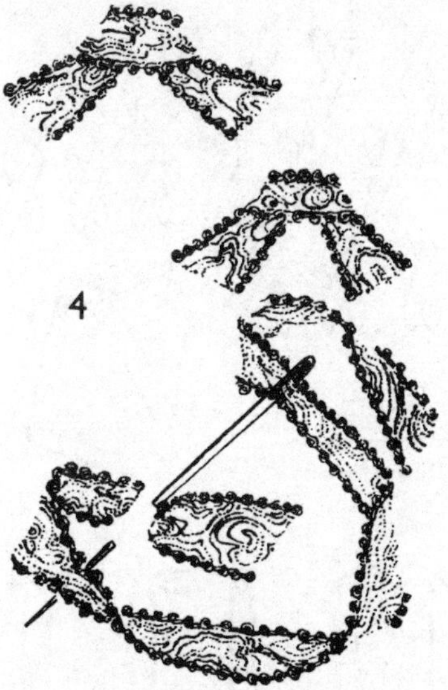

4

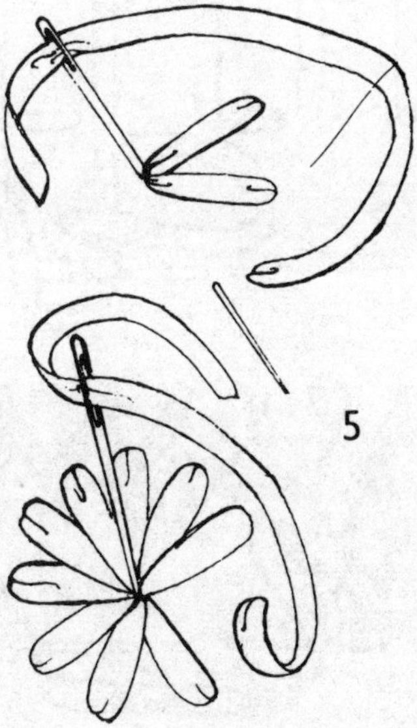

5

43

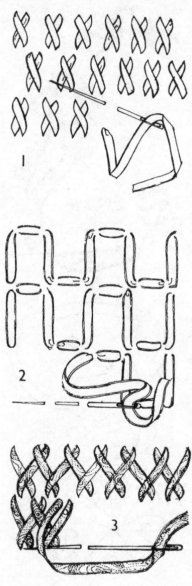

flower. Take care not to draw the ribbon too tightly as this will spoil its appearance, and also be sure not to let it get twisted. Finally bring the ribbon to the back of the fabric and secure with several catch stitches.

Ribbon Stitches. Many of the simpler decorative stitches explained at the beginning of the first chapter are easily adapted for stitched ribbon work. To start with $\frac{1}{4}''$ ribbon should be used with a wide eyed blunt pointed needle on slightly open weave fabric. Apart from bringing the ribbon through from the back of the fabric when starting and taking it to the back when finishing the ribbon is never taken completely through the fabric; instead it is passed under a few top threads as illustrated on the left.

1. **Cross Stitch.** Working from left to right bring the needle out $\frac{1}{4}''$ below the line to be worked. Make a stitch $\frac{1}{2}''$ above and $\frac{1}{4}''$ to the right of the first stitch, passing the needle between the fabric weave and bringing it out as shown by diagram 1. To complete the cross insert the needle $\frac{1}{2}''$ below the second stitch, bringing it out $\frac{1}{4}''$ to the right of the completed cross. Now work another complete cross by making a stitch from right to left by inserting the needle $\frac{1}{2}''$ above and $\frac{1}{4}''$ to the left of the ribbon, repeating stitch two, etc.

2. **Up & Down Stitch** is worked

from right to left as shown by diagram 2 on the left. First bring the thread out ¼″ above the line being worked. Make a double catch stitch ½″ below the first one by picking up just two top threads then passing the needle over the fabric for ¼″ and then picking up another two top threads as illustrated. Pull the ribbon through but not too

3. **Herringbone.** As can be seen in diagram 3 opposite, ribbon herringbone stitch is worked in exactly the same way as the embroidery herringbone stitch explained on page 9. Working from left to right pass your needle under several top threads and not right through the fabric. Make a second stitch ½″ above and ¼″ to the right of the first,

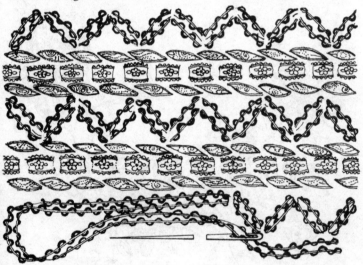

tightly, so that they lay neatly on the surface.

Next make another double catch stitch starting ½″ above the last one and again slotting the ribbon under two top threads then passing over ¼″ of fabric before picking up another two top threads, and then pull the ribbon through. Repeat stitches working several lines one above the other to get an all-over effect.

again picking up only a few top threads. Repeat the stitch ½″ below and ¼″ to the right, and then ½″ above etc. right along the line being worked. Make several lines with the top of one stitch being placed between two stitches of the previous line. Fancy ribbons can also be used, as shown above, interspacing picot edge herringbone ribbon stitch with jacquard ribbon running stitch and taffeta side stitch, etc. Try out several ideas before choosing which is the nicest for a particular job, as a little time spent experimenting often saves a lot of time unpicking.

Ribbon embroidery is best worked in softer ribbons than those used for ordinary slotted ribbon work as the ribbons are illustration below is a very good specimen of the kind of design which can be worked with soft ribbons. The bunches of flowers and leaves are all worked in the ribbon with the exception of the stems, which are normal embroidery stem stitch, as explained on page 9. The colours of the ribbons can be as bright or as

intended to crinkle slightly in the finished design, giving a natural softness to the design. Many ground fabrics can be used with a preference for firmer rather than softer ones, a thin lining of cotton being used as a backing for thin fabrics to give greater support to the ribbon embroidery. The design seen in our controlled as those used in other forms of embroidery, varying according to personal preference or the availability of colours. We suggest two shades of orange, one each of blue and yellow, two of pink and two of green, the fabric being heliotrope linen and the needle a wide oval eyed blunt-pointed chenille or similar type of needle.

The flowers and leaves are worked as shown, with the green ribbon being used for the leaves, the flowers being worked with alternate petals of the two shades of orange for the large blooms and one shade only of pink, yellow, blue and orange being used according to taste, with the tiny flowers being alternate light and dark orange.

The flower petals and leaves are made in the way shown on the right, taking care not to draw the ribbon too tightly, as that spoils its appearance, and also be sure not to let it get twisted. If two colours are used in the same blossom, go all round the flower with one colour, leaving room between the petals for the next shade, which is then added using the same stitch, as detailed on page 43.

To complete the design embroider the stems with stem stitch as explained on page 9, or use couch-stitched cording as on page 41. The smaller leaves can either be made by single stitches of green ribbon, used in the same way as working the petals shown on page 43, or just two embroidery stitches one longer than the other, placed side by side.

When the flowers are finished, make several green bullion stitches in the middle of each, as shown on page 15. Finally the back of the work can be ironed using a slightly damp cloth and warmish iron.

Gathered ribbon flowers are simple to make, yet offer considerable variety by the use of different colours, textures and widths of ribbon.

1. To make the flower shown below cut a piece of ribbon $\frac{3}{4}''$ wide and $6''$ long as in diagram 1, trimming the ends diagonally. Run a gathering stitch from the couched stem, cut-edge felt leaves and stem stitching as required. These flowers could be made into bunches or they could be scattered at random. Change the size and colours according to your personal preference.

Ribbon Rose. To make the generously proportioned rose illustrated on the right you will

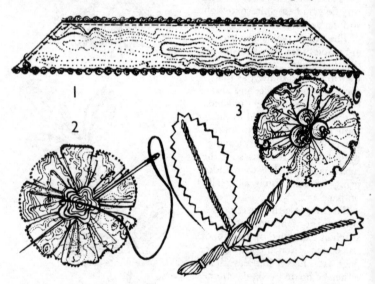

point along the right-hand diagonal across the shorter side and up the left diagonal.

2. Draw up the gathering thread and arrange the ribbon neatly, overlapping the ends and then sewing through the centre edges at the back as shown in diagram 2.

3. Stitch the ribbon flower into position, adding coloured bead or bullion-stitched centres,

require $1\frac{1}{2}$ yds of $1\frac{1}{2}''$ wide ribbon. First cut a petal pattern out of thin cardboard from a cornflakes box or something similar. The pattern should be the shape of the petal before it is gathered up as in diagram 4, and should measure $5''$ long and $1\frac{1}{2}''$ wide, or the width of the ribbon, with the ends being cut diagonally for $1''$. Next cut the ribbon into petal sections using the cardboard template as a guide, so that all the petals are exactly alike, turning the template up and down so that diagonals interlock, thus avoiding any undue wastage. Gather up each petal, starting at the extreme point, running along the diagonal to the shorter side, then straight across and up

towards the centre to give the effect shown, sewing them on securely to the ground fabric, but avoiding a stiff effect. As you approach the centre arrange the petals closer together to give the effect of the centre of the rose, and helping to conceal the raw edges underneath.

If a two-colour rose is required

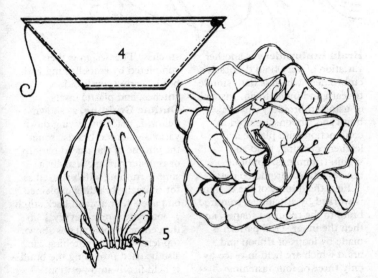

the other diagonal, drawing them up to about $1\frac{1}{4}''$. This may be done by hand or machine. Now join the individual petals, which should look like diagram 5, into one continuous strip by machine-stitching over the gathering, adding one petal at a time.
Mark out a $2\frac{1}{2}''$ circle and arrange the petals in spiral fashion use

1 yard of $1\frac{1}{2}''$ ribbon for the outside petals and $\frac{1}{2}$ yard of $1''$ ribbon of a different shade for the inside petals, varying the textures or colour as required.

Add cordwork or couching as explained on page 40/41, ribbon embroidery as on page 46, turned edge appliqué as on page 62, or any of the other techniques that interests you.

49

Braid Embroidery is another variation of very bold decorative embroidery which is both simple to learn and quick to do. Instead of using embroidery threads braid and ribbons are used in conjunction with plastic and leather couching, bead and sequin trimmings, appliqué centres and embroidered details.

First the outline of the design is worked by stitching a coloured braid to the required shapes, and then the inner scroll pattern is made by loops of ribbon and braid which are held in place by only three or four fastening stitches. The design is then completed by embellishing with beads, various embroidery stitches, and plastic insets.

Outline Braiding, as shown below, is made by sewing down various coloured braids around the outline of the traced pattern or transfer design. Usually a simple running stitch is used as for soutache braiding explained on page 88, or a small back stitch $\frac{1}{8}''$ long and worked every $\frac{3}{8}''$ in the centre of the braid as shown top left. Machine stitching can also be used providing the braid is held firmly into position.

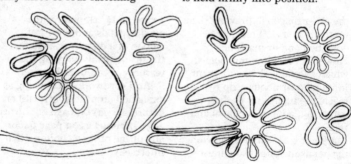

At the curves of the design ease the braid smoothly around the outside edge so that the inside is slightly full. The curves can then be pressed into shape.

Braid Flowers, as shown below, are made by looping lengths of coloured braid and ribbons into various patterns, and then

the ends. The whole design is then completed by stitching lengths of cord or braid between each looped section with some additional couching and embroidery stitches as desired.

Braided Appliqué. Various coloured shapes of felt and fabrics can also be used in

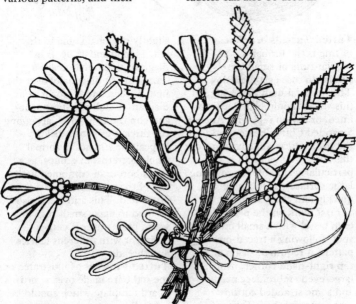

securing each loop with several hand stitches at both top and bottom. The looped flowers are then decorated with beads and embroidery stitches as illustrated on the top right-hand corner of the opposite page. The ears of corn are even more quickly made, a single stitch on the top fold forms the beard, whilst a smaller stitch is used at the junction of

conjunction with braid embroidery and braid flowers. These appliqué shapes are first of all roughly edge-stitched into position and then the raw edges are covered and permanently fixed by outlining the design in braid, cord and couching as shown on pages 60 and 61, before adding bead and embroidery embellishments.

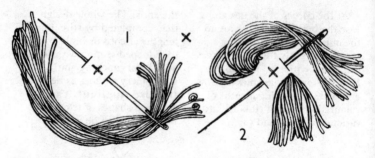

Tufted Tassals or Maltese tufting is the formal use of regular tufts or small tassels, similar to those shown below. The material used for trying out this stitch should be a fairly firm linen, or cotton rep, with Anchor Stranded Cotton being used for the tufts. Once you have tried out this stitch you will find it particularly suitable for covering large surfaces, as it can be quickly and easily done.

First mark on the places for each tassel with a small cross or spot, following a traced-on pattern if required. Begin at the top right-hand corner, using a large-eyed embroidery needle and some stranded cotton embroidery thread. Take a slightly diagonal stitch to the left, $\frac{1}{4}''$ long and $\frac{1}{8}''$ up as in diagram 1, and then make a second stitch diagonally over the first, $\frac{1}{4}''$ long and $\frac{1}{8}''$ down as in diagram 2. Pull the stitch taut and clip the ends to $\frac{1}{2}''$, arranging the threads as shown below. Repeat the stitches in formal single patterns, in groups, as a tassel border or combined with any of the other methods illustrated. This stitch can also be used to make small rugs or a warm pram cover if you experiment with different fabrics and threads.

Tufted Flowers as illustrated on the right are made over a cardboard template which should be cut to the size and shape required.

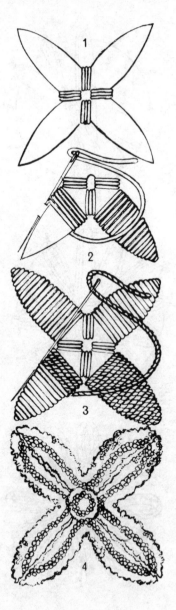

Start by cutting a template out of stiffish card—cardboard from a cereal packet is ideal. If you are making an irregular random design then free-hand cut templates are used, but if you are planning a formal arrangement accurate templates are required. Try making several experimental shapes before deciding, trying out the shape in coloured wool on a firm fabric before starting an ambitious design.

1. Place the card template into position and stitch over the edge and through the hole to secure it firmly into place with coloured wool.

2. Work first along one petal making $\frac{1}{8}$" wide stitches, first on one side looping across to the other side and then back again until completely covered.

3. Having covered the template with loops of coloured wool you can now work another colour over the top in a similar way.

4. Starting from the centre of the template cut the coloured wool loops along the centre of each petal so that the strands open out like the petal of a flower and the template can then be removed.

5. If required the tufting strands can now be secured from behind with some oversewing, using matching coloured cottons, or they can be secured before cutting.

Looped Rosettes can be easily made on a special Wendy multi-needle rosette winder which can be purchased from most sewing

53

shops. It is very simple to use
and has the added advantage of
being very quick. These looped
rosettes can be made separately
for incorporating with one of the
other methods explained in this
chapter, or for use with appliqué
and embroidery, or they can be
joined together to make complete
garments or bedspreads in a
similar way to crochet.

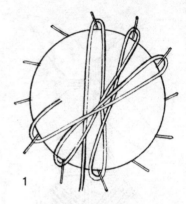

1

1. To make an open-centred
round rosette wind a half to one
yard of wool around the prongs
from one side to the other,
progressing in a clockwise
direction as shown on the left
until all the prongs have been
looped twice.

2. Cut the remaining wool to
10″ and thread it on to a wide-
eyed needle. Make a stitch in the
centre of the rosette and draw
out between two petals. Bring
the needle over and down into
the centre again and draw out
between the next set of petals,
working clockwise until all the
loops are enclosed.

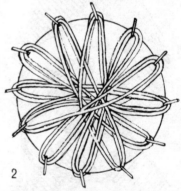

2

Many other looped rosette
designs can be made with the
Wendy Winder including square
rosettes, closed edge rosettes,
beaded rosettes, and rosettes with
pom-pom centres. They can also
be made in a continuous strip,
using coloured string, embroidery
thread, plastic or leather strips,
crochet cotton or many other
types of thread that you care to
experiment with and which turns
out into a interesting and usable
rosette.

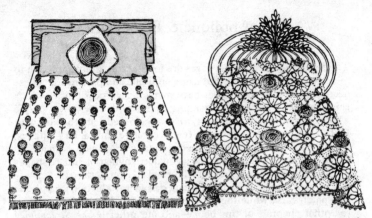

On this page are just a few ideas for bedspreads which can be made using the various techniques explained in this chapter. These are just some of the many, many ways of decorating bed covers and spreads. Some are extremely simple and quick and can be easily made by even the most inexperienced needle-woman.

As with all other kinds of sewing, before you start making,

spend a little time looking around the shops and stores, magazines and newspapers, collecting as many notes and press cuttings as possible so that these can be used in much the same way as cooking recipes. However, avoid getting involved in the usual mumbo-jumbo of traditional craft technique; instead choose bold methods that can be quickly made in striking colours with interesting but simple patterns.

3. Appliqué & Patchwork

The following twenty-four pages are intended as an introduction to the many ways of making and using appliqué and patchwork. These decorative sewing techniques have many design possibilities which can be made in many ways, ranging from simple stuck-on appliqué which is made with boldly cut areas of coloured felt stuck on with UHU and strengthened with a few decorative embroidery stitches, to the more complicated geometric patchwork which is made by using accurately cut lozenge, hexagonal, triangular or square shapes of fabric oversewn together into a formal all over pattern.

The methods explained are intended as an introduction to appliqué and patchwork, while the general methods of decorative sewing in the other chapters of this book—and our other books *Streamlined Dressmaking, Streamlined Curtains and Covers,* and *Streamlined Sewing for Fun*—are intended to be combined together and liberally interpreted to help you make decorative things of your own design.

Appliqué. This form of surface decoration is made by sticking and stitching various cut out pieces of differently coloured fabrics on to a contrasting background, and then enriching and unifying the design with embroidery, braiding and linking stitches. Success depends as much on the boldness of the design as it does on the complementing or contrasting use of both colour and texture as well as the neatness of the stitching.

As with all other kinds of decorative sewing, first spend a little time looking around the shops and stores, in magazines and newspapers, collecting as many notes and cuttings as possible so that these can be used in much the same way as cooking recipes. However, do remember to avoid getting involved in the off-putting techniques of traditional needlework. Instead opt for the simplest methods, interesting patterns, gay colours and attractive designs, so that your sewing will be easy and quick to do.

Cut and stitched appliqué is best used on firmish non-frayable material which can be safely cut to shape and then either hand-stitched as shown on the right, or machine-stitched around the raw edges. The appliqué can then be decorated with couching outlines, braid or rick-rack, chain stitching and various embroidery stitches, as shown on pages 14, 18, 40, 50, etc. etc.

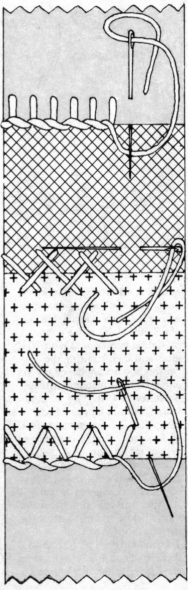

cut method for thin frayable fabrics.

First cut a template of stiffish paper the exact size and shape required—pages from a glossy monthly magazine or card from a cereal packet are ideal—then cut a piece of fabric $\frac{1}{4}''$ to $\frac{3}{8}''$ larger than the template. Next turn the edges over the paper template and crease them flat with a warm iron, tacking any difficult edges to hold accurately. After pressing the turnings flat remove the paper template and any tacking, then slip-stitch into position—or use blanket stitch, side stitch, machine stitching, etc. Finally, boldly decorate with areas of embroidery stitches, beading, couching and braid-

Stuck & stiched felt appliqué is the simplest form of appliqué and only entails sticking cut-outs of coloured felt on to a contrasting fabric background with UHU glue, and then securing the centres and occasional edges with either hand or machine stitches.

Stitched & Cut. This method is used on thin fabrics which easily fray if cut to shape before appliquéing. Simply cut a larger area of fabric than is needed, marking the exact shape required using dressmaking chalk; this is then machine zig-zag or hand-stitched through on to the main fabric before trimming away the surplus fabric edges.

Turned Edge. The turned-in method of appliqué is used as an alternative to the stitched and

work, etc., as shown on various other pages in this and our companion books.

Cut-Outs. This is a sort of reversed appliqué, with the stitched edge being worked on the main body fabric. The centre fabric shape is then cut away leaving a hole which is then backed up in different coloured fabrics, slotted ribbons, embroidery mirrors, plastic pieces, patterned braids, etc.

Inlaid appliqué is another variation of appliqué work, but instead of overlaying the various fabric pieces to form a design, the inlaid appliqué pieces are set into the main body of fabric using the stitches explained on pages 22 and 72. The inlaying of

coloured felt is the most successful form of inlaid appliqué work although other non-frayable materials can also be used.

First an accurate paper shape must be cut which is then marked on to the main body fabric. Next an identically sized marking must be made on to the contrasting fabric. Cut away the centre of the body fabric and trim the contrasting fabric to size. Now simply slot the contrasting inlaid section into the main cut-out fabric and link-stitch together. The cut-out section can now be used to set into another colour, and the design develops by counterchanging the piece so that there is no wastage. Sections of turned edge fabric can also be used.

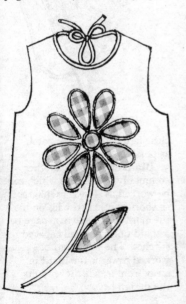

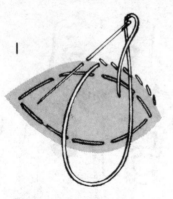

I

is just less than ⅛″ from the edge.
Make the second stitch ⅛″ above
and ⅛″ to the left, and bring the
needle out ⅛″ away from the first
stitch so that it is just under ⅛″
in from the edge as shown.

2. **Chain Stitch** is one of the
many novelty stitches which can
be used to attach appliqué
motifs. The chain is made in
exactly the same way as explained
on page 12, and is worked as

Appliqué Stitches. It is
advisable to tack all the appliqué
motifs into place before stitching
on any of them. Usually some of
the sections overlap one another;
if this happens trim away as
much of the underlapping motifs
as possible to avoid too many
thicknesses.

1. **Side Stitch.** The most
commonly used stitch for
attaching appliqué is the simple
side stitch shown in diagram 1.
Start by bringing the needle
through on the right hand corner
of the appliqué motif so that it

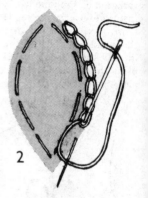

2

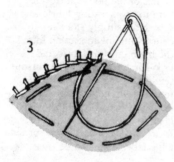

3

close to the edge of the patch
as possible.

3. **Blanket stitch** is another
commonly used stitch which can
be worked as shown in diagram 3
as short slanting stitches on to
the motif or, as shown on page 10,
as bold upright evenly spaced
stitches. The stitch can be
worked towards the motif or
away from it, whichever suits
the design best.

4. Couched Appliqué follows much the same sewing methods explained for simple cut and stitched appliqué with the addition of a coloured couching cord or decorative strip being introduced with the side or blanket stitch as shown by diagrams 4 below and on the right, turning to pages 17 and 41 for additional sewing information about other forms or couching.

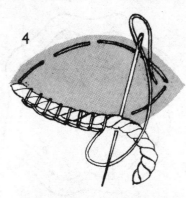

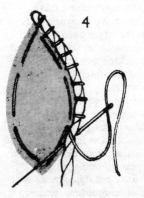

motifs already explained. The first essential is to tack the various motifs into position so that they can be easily machine-stitched around all the inter-linking edges with a minimum of stoppages. If you are lucky enough to have an automatic swing-needle sewing machine you will find that you can choose from a wide range of easy to make embroidery stitches which can be used on most appliqué work. Many interesting designs can be worked out even by the beginner provided the appliqué is bold enough.

5. Buttonhole stitch can be used for attaching and neatening the edges of very frayable material motifs which have not been turned under. The stitch can either be worked as shown on the right as a close blanket stitch or it can be worked like a normal buttonhole as shown on page 106.
6. Machine appliqué is made in much the same way as the various hand stitched appliqué

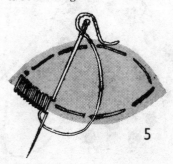

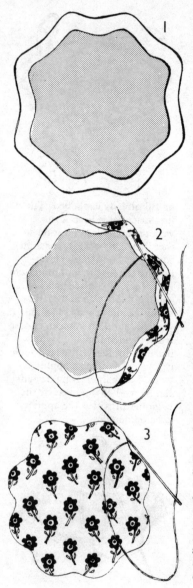

Shaped Appliqué. To make an intricately shaped turned edge motif out of thin frayable material it is best to proceed as follows.

1. First cut an accurate template the exact size and shape required —the cover of a glossy monthly magazine or card from a cereal packet is ideal—then cut a piece of fabric $\frac{1}{4}''$ to $\frac{3}{8}''$ larger than the template as shown by diagram 1 on the left.

2. Next place the card template on to the back of the fabric leaving an even turning all round. Turn the edges over the card and crease them flat with a warm iron, tacking any difficult edges to hold accurately as shown in diagram 2.

3. After pressing the turnings flat remove the card template and any tackings, then slip-stitch into position as in diagram 3, or use side stitch or blanket stitch as explained on page 60.

4. Finally boldly decorate with areas of embroidery stitches, beads, couching and braidwork, using traditional skeins of Anchor Stranded Cotton, some Tapisserie wool, Perlita, knitting wools, raffia, strands of leather and plastic, ribbons, russia braid, crochet thread, rug wool, and even coloured string, etc., as explained on pages 32, 40, 46, 51 and elsewhere in this book.

Appliqué Cushions. There are about as many different ways of designing and making appliqué cushions as there are people sewing, for cushions can be all sorts of shapes and sizes, covered in all sorts of fabrics, decorated with all kinds of different surface treatments, and made with various technical methods. The only guiding principle is, if the cushion looks right and is either useful or decorative, then it is a good cushion. A beautifully sewn but ugly or uncomfortable cushion is far better forgotten, by designing and making another one to take its place.

Cushion making. To make a simple appliqué cushion first cut two identical rectangles of fabric and appliqué the chosen design on to the right side of one of them. Next lay the rectangle of fabric together face to face with edges exactly matching. Stitch all round $\frac{1}{2}''$ in, leaving a turning through opening 6″ long in the middle of one side.

Turn cushion through this gap so that the fabric and appliqué is right side out, and then fill with kapok, polythene cuttings, or similar inexpensive filling before slip-stitching the gap edges together.

If the cushion is one of a group similar to the garden cushions illustrated on the right then it is best to make a paper pattern for the basic rectangular shape so that each cushion is made the correct size.

Appliqué Pictures or wall-hangings can be made in many ways, from the simple felt stuck-and-stitched nursery

picture shown below, the companion picture cushions shown opposite and on page 63, to an intricately worked family portrait. The materials which can be used include a mixture of coloured and textured fabrics and felts, braids and beads, raffia, coloured wools, and strands

you choose. The only criterion is whether you, your family and your friends like the finished article, and if it looks right in the room for which it was designed.

Before you start making an appliqué picture spend a little time looking through some nicely

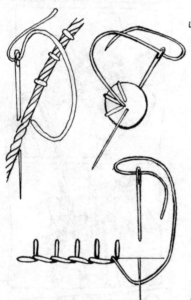

of leather and plastic, in fact anything that takes your fancy.

As explained earlier, the choice of design is unlimited, as there are no hard and fast rules governing the sewing techniques. It you enjoy experimenting you can make an appliqué design in any way, and by any method,

illustrated books. If you are making a nursery picture look through Kate Greenaway's illustrations for *Mother Goose*, one of Dick Bruna's Christmas books, or some of Gallery Five's gift or party cards.

If you wish to make something more sophisticated then look at one of Edmund Dulac's picture books, or if you would like to make an 'op-pop' art or space-age-inspired design you could work from a *Dr. Who's Weekly*. Having looked at these various illustrations try putting different pleasing shapes and interesting textures together to get a feel of

pictures interesting, rather than the less imaginative and laboured copying line-for-line of a Rubens or Van Gogh.

Try experimenting with different techniques, combining braid and ribbon work, explained on pages 46 and 51, with stuck and stitched appliqué work from

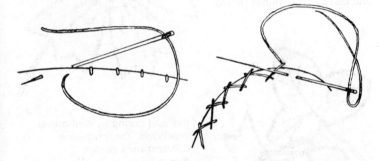

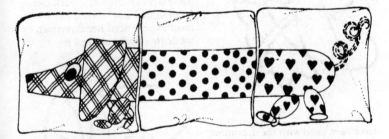

the design, shifting the cut-outs around to obtain the best design balance before sewing them into place. These designs should be your own personal creation, and not simply sewn copies of other people's artworks, for it is the personal touch and variation on an idea which makes appliqué

page 58, or embroidery stitches from page 14 with some beading from page 34 and tufting from page 53.

Start by roughing out your design with coloured felt-tipped pens on to a sheet of wrapping paper, adding an assortment of felt and fabric cut-outs and other extras as required. Also try making your own fringed hem as shown on page 102. In fact try anything which encourages you to sew. But remember that whatever your final choice, your appliqué work must be interesting to look at, and have bold colours and exciting textures, and that all these things should

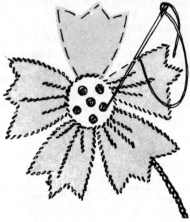

dull and boring by continuous repetition. Try something different for a change.

Experimental Appliqué and decorative embroidery work can be designed and worked out by most experienced needlewomen, while those who are less ex-

have been used with the maximum of ease and pleasure and the minimum of skill and trouble. For a picture which is beautifully sewn but dull in design or over-laboured is far better forgotten by making another to take its place.

As you can see, your scope is quite unlimited, so remember, never let your sewing become design. Also explained are the various sewing needles to use and what embroidery threads to buy. However, once you have a little experience at this kind of decorative sewing you can try some experiments of your own, choosing different colour combinations or different thread textures to suit your own design ideas. Traditionally the em-

perienced can buy extremely good transfer designs from most embroidery shops. These transfer designs are ironed on to the fabric as a guide to the appliqué motifs and stitching details, which are fully explained in the instruction leaflet sold with the

broidery stitches are worked in skeins of Anchor stranded cotton, tapisserie wool or Perlita, as these can be bought at most shops in a wide range of colours, but it can be great fun to supplement them with knitting wool, raffia, strands of leather and plastic, ribbons, russia braid, crochet thread, rug wool, coloured string, old buttons,

67

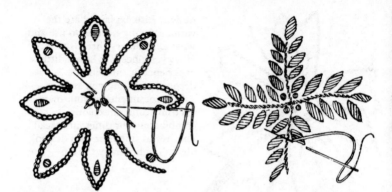

curtain rings, beads and sequins, etc., etc. It is important to re-emphasise the importance of not getting bogged down with the usual mumbo-jumbo of traditional sewing methods and the usual choice of decorative threads. For needlework need not be such a laborious chore as the traditionalists make it sound. Instead, be as creative as you can by using simple patterns, interesting but not necessarily intricate designs and striking colours and trimmings, using sewing methods which are easy and straightforward with no inhibiting rules. You will then find that your decorative sewing will not only be quick and easy to do, but also thoroughly enjoyable and fun as well.

Appliqué toys, party bibs, fancy dress or beach clothes and children's presents should be bold and colourful, using big

details, unusual trimmings and interesting extras, forgetting as much as possible the intricate details and subtleties of fine sewing. The designs shown on the right and those on pages 30, 58, 63, 65 and 110, etc. are only intended to illustrate the range of designs which can be made for both boys and girls. Many more can easily be made by those who like to experiment; ideas range from traditional Christmas stockings to a space-age Cosmonaut's outfit.

Party bib. To make the party bib shown on the right you will require a 9″ × 12″ rectangle of cotton fabric, 1 yard of edging lace, some coloured bias binding for the neck, some ribbon for the bow, and some odd scraps of coloured felt, patterned fabric and other trimmings for the appliqué work. Mark out the neck shape with the aid of a cocoa tin and round off the corner with a saucer, trimming the raw edges with the lace and binding the neck with bias strip. Boldly design and stitch the appliqué pattern and finally add a pretty ribbon each side of the neck for tying into an attractive bow.

Nursery Cushions. To make a nursery cushion as shown on the right follow the general making and designing techniques explained on pages 62 and 63 However, do avoid using any easily detachable trimmings as these could be a potential danger

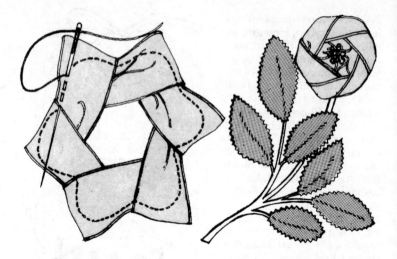

to very young children. Generally speaking it is better to concentrate on large bold areas in striking colour combinations rather than intricately sewn details. For instance the cow-shaped cushion shown overleaf is simply a normal 10″ square cushion made in cream-coloured corduroy with contrasting patches of soft leather or felt, hand-stitched on, an embroidered fabric and felt head filled with kapok, stuffed fabric legs and a rug-wool tassel for the tail.

A lot of other interesting and unusually shaped designs—such as a pig, snail, or owl-shaped cushion toys—can be made quite successfully by first roughing out the shape on a sheet of wrapping paper, experimenting with coloured felt-tipped pens, and adding an assortment of felt and fabric cut-outs and other extras, in much the same way as explained for appliqué pictures on pages 65 and 66.

Another possibility, instead of filling the cushion with kapok, is to sew a 6″ zip fastener on to the turning through gap so that it can be used for a nightie case.

As with other sewing always be on the look-out for new ideas, for novelty is of great importance, and remember to note in your scrap-book any idea you see in the magazines or newspapers, on television or in your local toyshop, for the possibilities are endless, and the scope for original or improvised design is enormous. **Appliqué flowers** made of ribbon and satin combined with chiffon and cording, with felt-work leaves and beaded centres, and embellished with an assortment of embroidery stitches and added extras, makes an exciting addition to normal appliqué work. The flowers can be as simple as the one shown on the left or they can be grouped together as illustrated below.

To make a simple ribbon rose cut six pieces of 1″ ribbon, each 2″ long, and arrange them into an overlapping circle as shown on the left, sewing around the circle to hold them into position. Draw the gathering thread quite tight and fasten securely by oversewing several times across the gathering. Now make another blossom using 2½″ long pieces of ribbon, but do not draw the gathering thread quite so tightly. Next slip the first flower inside the larger one and fasten the two together by stab stitching through the centre, adding a few beads as centre stamens. Finally cut some felt leaves, pinking the edges, and add couched cord stems and embroidered veining.

Other flowers can be made by varying the ribbons or alternating the petal colours and combining them with the ribbon work flowers shown on pages 46 to 49, and the cordwork ones on page 51, adding small pom-poms and other extras as required.

Patchwork, like appliqué, has many variations, ranging from the very traditional designs in formal prints to op-art irregularity with psychedelic colouring.

In order to achieve the effect required some thought must be given to the choice of fabrics to those used together are of a similar type. However, do not mix washable and non-washable fabrics for articles that have to be laundered.

Except for crazy patchwork, in which the fabric pieces are all shapes and sizes, the designs

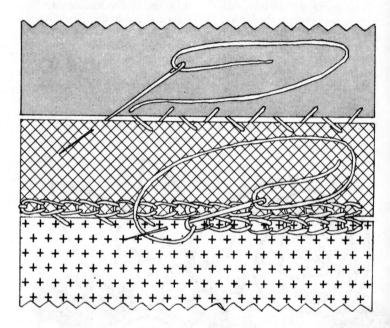

be used, as a certain mixing of colour and texture is necessary. The use of plain and patterned fabric in juxtaposition will be given an entirely different effect from the use of all-patterned or all-plain fabrics.

Almost any material is suitable for most patchwork, providing should be built up with geometrical shapes that will fit into each other, so that when they are used one with another they give a variety of patterns.

Patchwork can also be combined with appliqué, ribbon work, embroidery, and many of the other types of surface decoration explained in the other chapters of this book.

Felt Patchwork is the simplest form of patchwork to make as no turning under of the fabric raw edges is required. The felt should be cut into interlocking sections using accurate templates for marking the squares, triangles, or diamond shapes required. These interlocking shapes are then sewn together using the simple stitch shown on the left which is worked over and under the edge as illustrated, giving a fish-bone effect, The fish-bone seam can then be decorated with chain stitch as shown by the lower diagram on the left or by one of the many other embroidery stitches explained in the first chapter. Alternatively one of the more decorative insertion stitches shown on the right can be used, also those on pages 22 and 23.

Diagram 1 shows a linking buttonhole stitch which is worked in groups of three or four stitches one each side. Blanket stitch can be used in a similar way.

Diagram 2 is a stitch which is made alternately top and bottom in the same way as explained for the simple fish-bone stitch above. When working the stitch pass the needle through the looped thread as shown.

Diagram 3 is a zig-zag knotted stitch which is made by passing the needle under and through the looped thread as shown before making a diagonal stitch to the opposite side.

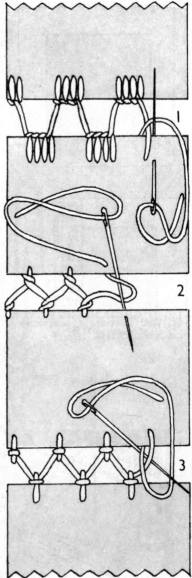

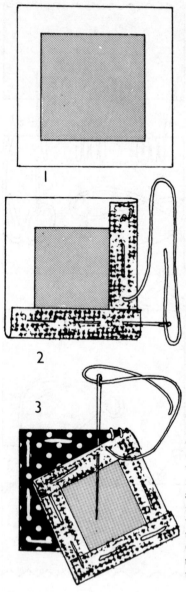

Traditional Patchwork. The most suitable materials for the traditional forms of patchwork are plain and printed cotton fabrics, although some medium weight silks, velvets, needlecords and even thin woollen fabrics can be used. However, it is always best to keep to one type of material if possible to prevent the patches from pulling each other out of shape.

Next you will need to buy or make some accurately shaped templates, the most popular shapes being squares, rectangles, triangles, diamonds, hexagons and octagons, with shell or fish scale shapes being an interesting alternative. The bought templates are usually in metal or plastic, or you can make your own in stiff card if you can cut them perfectly accurate. As a guide for cutting the material a larger cardboard shape is a great help. This should be cut $\frac{1}{4}''$ larger all round than the patchwork template.

Using the fabric cutting guide cut several dozen pieces of differently coloured or varying patterned cotton fabrics, then cut the same number of pieces of paper using the correct patch-work template—old glossy magazine pages are ideal. Place a paper shape on to the wrong side of a cut shape of fabric and turn the edges over all round, tacking the turnings flat. Complete all the pieces cut in this way and then join the pieces together, laying two shapes edge to edge with the right sides of the fabric facing and hand-stitch together, being careful not to leave any gaps. Lay another shape on to the second and stitch together, then a fourth.

Next place one patch under the first and then another patch under the second, and so on until you have sewn all the pieces into a 'block'. Make several

that all corners are neatly and accurately turned in.

Diagram 3 shows the stitch used for joining one piece of fabric to the next, taking care not to leave any gaps and to conceal the stitches as much as possible from the right side.

Diagram 4 is a variation of diagram 2 for turning in and tacking hexagon patchwork

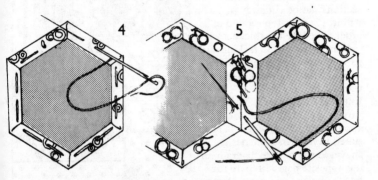

blocks in this way before joining them all together into the finished shape. Finally remove the tacking stitches and inner paper shapes before pressing.

Diagram 1 shows the accurately cut paper shape being placed on the wrong side of the cut fabric, leaving an even $\frac{1}{4}''$ turning all round.

Diagram 2 illustrates the method used for folding over and tacking down the $\frac{1}{4}''$ edge finishing allowance. Make sure

shapes, taking care to fold each corner accurately.

Diagram 5 shows an alternative method for stitching the more intricately shaped patchwork sections together. Take care, however, that the needle only passes through the edges and does not show on the right side.

Applied Patchwork is a type of work in which patchwork shapes are arranged in an interesting design on to a contrasting background material,

75

as can be seen by the illustration on the right.

The patches are first cut out as for normal patchwork, then joined together in a geometric or irregular pattern. The outside edge of the motif is then turned under all round and then arranged into position on the background fabric and top- or slip-stitched all round.

If a number of the patches overlap each other the under sections can be cut away to within $\frac{1}{2}''$ of the top section in order to reduce the thicknesses.

Finally remove all tacking and paper shapes before pressing with a damp cloth and medium warm iron.

Lapped Patchwork. This is a variation on traditional and applied patchwork which is most suited to the fish-scale design shown in the middle diagram on the opposite page. Prepare the fabric sections and paper shapes as explained before, but instead of creasing over all the turnings just fold over and tack around the top curve, leaving the rest of the turnings free. Lay four scales face up with the creased-over top curves facing away from you, and their corners overlapping $\frac{1}{4}''$. Lay four more patchwork scales below these so that the top of the curve just laps $\frac{1}{4}''$ over the lower turnings of the first row of scales.

Pin the intersections together and tack through the second row of top curves through the underlap allowances. Either turn to back

76

Brick Patchwork

Fish-scale Patchwork

Crazy Patchwork

and hand-stitch the lapped edges together, taking care that no stitches show on the right side, or top-stitch neatly into blocks before joining more scale sections together.

Crazy Patchwork. Either the traditional or the lapped method of patchwork can be used to join the pieces together, providing accurately cut pieces of inter-locking paper templates are first prepared. An easy method of preparation is to draw out the irregular design required on to a sheet of cheap cartridge paper, cut along each line, having numbered the pieces to aid reassembly, and then cut the fabric pieces $\frac{1}{4}''$ larger all round than the paper pieces. Next place the paper shape on to the wrong side of a fabric section and turn the edges over all round, tacking the turnings flat. Take the next patchwork shape and turn under all edges except the edge adjacent to the first section, which should be lap-stitched into position. The third shape is also tacked into shape except where the first and second sections overlap, which are then stitched into position. Proceed with tacking and lapping until the crazy patchwork is complete as shown on the left.

Patchwork Bedspreads. There are many different ways of making decorative bedspreads and covers. Most are extremely simple and can be easily made by the most inexperienced

77

needlewoman. Just a few methods are shown here and on page 55, but many other methods explained throughout this book can also be easily adapted to make your covers interesting.

Knitted Patchwork bedspreads, similar to the one shown below, can be made out of a number of 8″ or 9″ rectangles and squares made out of brightly coloured wool samplers using a variety of

together with openwork and crochet criss-cross chains. The circular motifs can be made in many varying patterns and sizes providing they form a unified design when stitched to the background fabric.

Patchwork motifs of a geometric design, as shown below, are made from a selection of brightly coloured and patterned cotton fabrics which are joined

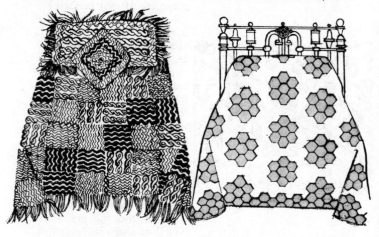

stitches. Simply sew the knitted samplers together forming a completely random pattern. Squares of crochet can also be used, as can coloured pieces of fabric sewn together with the knitting into a formal or crazy pattern.

Crochet Patchwork, as shown on page 55, can be made from circular motifs of crochet which are stitched to a backing of coloured lawn and then linked

together in the traditional way explained on page 74 and then either hand- or machine-stitched appliqué into a formal arrangement. Random or crazy patchwork can also be used in a similar way as shown on page 76.

Embroidered Patchwork, as shown on the right, and other ideas apart from those already mentioned in this chapter—maybe ideas of your own which incorporate unusual colourings, exciting textures and bold design details which do not have to conform to outdated rule—can be incorporated into your appliqué and patchwork.

The previous twenty-three pages will have given you an introduction into this form of decorative sewing, the general methods being intended to be liberally interpreted to help you develop original ideas of your own.

Part of the fun of sewing is creating and adapting all sorts of ideas, so it is worth spending a little time browsing through shops and stores, thumbing through magazines and news-papers, as well as noticing things in friends' houses and on TV to get ideas and to help crystallize your thoughts.

Collect together as many notes, press cuttings, pictures and samples of materials as possible so that whenever you are in the mood to create something new you will only have to refer to your scrap-book to find a wealth of ideas in much the same way as a book of cooking recipes helps when planning a meal. You will find that a scrap-book kept up-to-date will become just as important to your sewing as your scissors or pins.

It you think of your sewing in this way without any inhibiting rules you will find that it will not only be quick and easy to do, but will also be thoroughly enjoyable and fun as well.

4. Decorative Edges

In this chapter we shall explain some of the simplest ways of making all sorts of decorative edgings for use on curtains and blinds, bed-spreads and garden hammocks as well as for dressmaking, etc. Many of the design instructions are intended to be used as a basis from which to work and develop further ideas of your own, and we hope they will encourage you to attempt to make all sorts of things you have never tried before. With this in mind, and remembering that there are really no hard and fast rules to worry about, your efforts can be regarded as an exciting challenge rather than an exacting task.

Decorative edges can be made in many different ways using a variety of ready-made trimmings available at most large stores or specialist shops. Which type to use on a particular design depends partly on one's own particular taste, partly on the fabric used, partly on the design, and partly on the prevailing fashion. But as the basic idea is to enhance the general look of the design making it more interesting or adding a touch of originality, it should be remembered

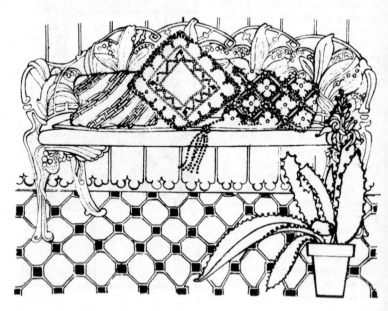

that to do this it should be well made, as irregular sewing will detract from rather than enhance the finished appearance.

Decorative Hems. This type of edge decoration is the easiest to apply as it involves very little preparation, and no pattern or structural changes, and is usually made on a completed or nearly completed article. The simplest method is to stick and stitch a ready-made string fringe or decorative bobble edging on to the edge of your window blind or bedspread, whilst the more adventurous scalloped and tasselled ends can be made from separate strips of matching or contrasting pieces of fabric, as explained below, or from beads, braid, cordings, ribbons or any of the many other decorative things illustrated in the other chapters of this book.

Scalloped Hems. Scallops and tassellated hems are made from two layers of fabric placed wrong sides together and cut to the exact length and depth required. Divide the length into equal sections and lightly mark in pencil the shape required, using a saucer or cardboard template as a marking guide. Machine stitch around the pencil line through both thicknesses of fabric and then trim away the surplus fabric to $\frac{1}{8}''$ before covering the raw edge with braid, crossway binding or any trimmings similar to those shown on this page, or elsewhere in this chapter.

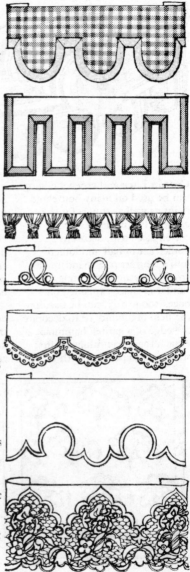

Cotton Lace and crochet edging can be used on many household items as well as things for the garden. For instance 6″ wide cotton lace strip, decorative doilies cut in half and joined into a long strip, or hand-made crochet edging and fringing similar to those explained on pages 100 to 103, can be used on the hem of a blind, or to decorate the edge of a garden hammock. Attach these trimmings by first sticking into position with UHU glue, lapping the edge by $\frac{1}{4}″$ to $\frac{1}{2}″$ and then stitching along the edge for extra strength.

Bobble Fringing and decorative cording can be stuck or stitched directly on to the bottom folded edge of many things ranging from a child's beach dress to a bedspread or lampshade.

Many fringings can also be purchased ready-made at most trimming counters in large department stores or you can experiment in making your own

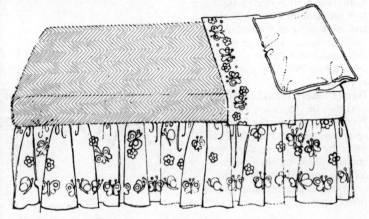

as explained for beaded fringing on page 33, soutache cording on page 88, knotted string work on page 103, or as seen in a current magazine article.

Applied decoration such as appliqué, embroidery, looped rosettes, pom-poms, or even felt and plastic stuck-ons, all of which are explained in the other sections of this book, can also be applied to the hems of many items, as can many other ideas seen in magazines and news-papers, in shops and on television. As new ideas are continually appearing on the market it is best to keep an open mind so that when you are deciding on what to use you will choose the best which is available now.

Stitched hems. Many decorative stitches can be used to hold a simple folded-under hem into position. Generally a hem is machine-stitched as shown on page 105, but if the edge is being decorated with some embroidery

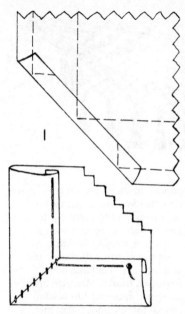

1

leaving a $\frac{1}{4}''$ seam allowance as shown. Refold the hem and side turnings, tack and slip-stitch the mitred edges together. Finally neaten the hem with one of the following decorative stitches or slip-stitch into position as shown on pages 104 and 105.

Chevron hemming stitch as illustrated below is worked from left to right. Begin by making a $\frac{1}{4}''$ long horizontal stitch through the top fabric and hem allowance as shown in diagram 2, bringing the needle out in the middle of the stitch. Next make a $\frac{1}{2}''$ long slanting stitch to the right passing the needle horizontally $\frac{1}{8}''$ to the left, then make the $\frac{1}{4}''$ long lower

stitches as shown on the right, then these stitches can be used to neaten the hem as well. Simply tack the hem up into position and work some of the embroidery stitches through the double thickness, catching the occasional gap with an extra slip stitch if required.

Hem corners should be mitred as shown by diagram 1 above. First fold and press the hem and open out the fold. Next fold and press the side turning allowance, and also open out. Now diagonally fold the corner inwards on the exact corner crease markings and then trim away the corner fold

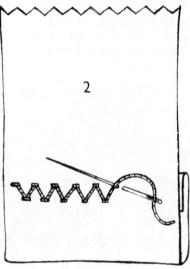

2

horizontal stitch, bringing the needle out in the middle of the stitch. Make the second slanting stitch upwards and then repeat the top horizontal stitch as already described, repeating the diagonal stitch every ½″.

Russian Interlacing as in diagram 3 below is worked in two separate journeys. The first process is to work an even row of herringbone stitch as explained on pages 8 and 9 through both the top layer of fabric and turned back hem allowance. The second row of stitches are worked in coloured thread and consist of horizontal stitches interlaced with the herringbone stitch as

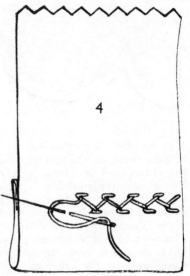

shown. Other interlacing stitches can also be used in this way, as shown on page 19, etc.

Ornamental Stitches such as the coral stitch shown in diagram 4 above can also be used for hemming. As illustrated this stitch is worked from right to left through both the top fabric and turned back hem allowance. Bring the needle up on the right, hold the thread lightly down with the left thumb, and make a short stitch ¼″ below and ¼″ to the left, keeping the thread under the needle point as in diagram 4. Draw up the thread and then make a similar stitch ¼″ above and

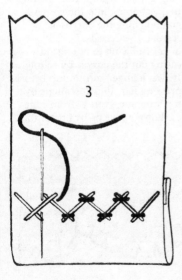

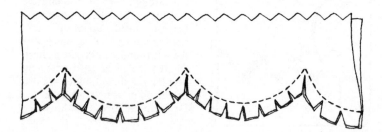

$\frac{1}{4}''$ to the left of the previous one with the needle passing over the loop of thread which is being held down by the left thumb. Continue working alternately above and below the previous stitch, fastening off the last with a back-stitch, after taking the thread through to the wrong side. **Faced hems** such as curves and scallops are made by stitching a strip of fabric around the required shape and then turning this strip on to the wrong side and then stitching flat in the normal way.
1. Cut a strip of stiffish paper the exact length of scalloped edge required. Divide the length into equal sections by measurement or by folding. Next roughly mark the first shape using a saucer, make-up jar or similar object as

a guide. Cut the first shape accurately and then use this to mark the second and third, etc.
2. Using the paper pattern as a guide mark the scallop shapes in HB pencil on to the wrong side of the fabric hem. Place a facing strip of fabric on to this edge with the right sides together and tack around the scallop markings.
3. Machine stitch around the markings as shown by the diagram below and trim turnings to $\frac{1}{8}''$, clipping into the corners and notching the curves at regular $\frac{1}{4}''$ intervals.
4. Turn facing to wrong side, easing out the curves by rolling between finger and thumb before pressing flat. Finish scallops by top stitching $\frac{1}{4}''$ to $\frac{3}{8}''$ from edge as shown above or by one of the

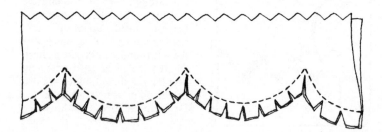

other decorative methods explained previously in this chapter.

Drawnwork. As explained on page 24 there are many decorative stitches used in drawn thread work which are usually made on linen fabrics or evenly woven materials of a similar type. The first process is to withdraw the threads carefully, cutting across the required number and withdrawing them gradually with the aid of a pin, until the correct width of open work is ready for stitching, interlacing and bar weaving, etc.

Openwork is another form of decorative stitching which can be used on the edges of many articles made out of even weave fabrics such as linen, muslin, lawn and organdie. Unlike drawn thread work explained above no threads are pulled out as the openwork is formed by drawing the fabric threads together with geometrically worked stitches.

Cutwork is a very distinctive form of stitched hem work which is ideally suited for decorative table linen, bedspreads, etc. Basically it consists of motifs which are surrounded by buttonhole or machine zig-zag stitches with the in-between areas being cut away. As explained on pages 26 and 27 occasional surface stitchery is added to enhance the finished look, giving this type of cut work a distinctive decorative richness as can be seen by the illustration on the right.

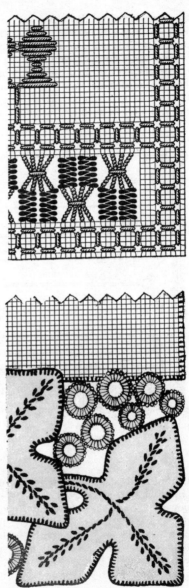

Soutache braid embroidery is a very decorative and useful type of bold stylized embroidery. The work is easily done and very effective when used in dressmaking, on cushions and bedspreads, or if stitched on to net as blind lace as shown below.

worked every $\frac{3}{8}''$ in the centre of the cord, or a simple running stitch. At the curves of the pattern ease the braid smoothly around the shape so that the inside edge is slightly full. This fullness can then be pressed to shrink the braided curve into

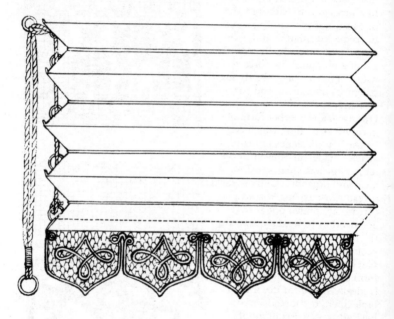

Outline cording, as illustrated opposite, is made by sewing down the soutache cord around the outline of the traced pattern or transfer design. The stitch used is either a machine stitch if you can hold the braid accurately, a small back stitch $\frac{1}{8}''$ long and

shape. As explained for couched embroidery on page 41, the ends of the braid must be threaded through to the wrong side of the fabric with the aid of a stiletto to make a small hole and a crochet hook to draw the braid through, securing the ends with

a few extra stitches.

Soutache Lace. Soutache braid embroidery on net makes very effective bold lace for trimming window blinds as shown opposite, or for valances, curtain edgings, or dress trimmings. Net of any kind and in every shade can be used, with braid in a corresponding colour or to contrast.

The design chosen is first copied on to a strip of stout brown paper, then the net is carefully tacked over the pattern. Next place the braid over the outline of the design and sew to the net, using a normal machine stitch, stitching through braid, net and paper.

Alternatively stitch by hand using an even running stitch through the centre of the braid and net, but avoiding the backing paper. Do not pull the stitches tightly as this tends to pucker the braid. When all the outline has been gone over, cut the tacking threads and remove the backing paper, re-using the design for the next section of net to be stitched. When complete press the back of the lace with a moderately warm iron and then trim away any unwanted net close to the braided outline. Finally embellish with a few crochet motifs or embroidery stitches if required.

Shop fringing made of twisted string, looped art silk or fluffy pom-poms can be stuck and stitched on to the hems and edges of most things from bath-mats and cushions to nursery pictures or rag dolls. Generally there is a large range of ready-made edge trimmings available at most notion counters in the larger stores or specialist sewing shops or you can make your own as explained on pages 100 to 103. To attach these made or bought fringes you should first stick them to the edges, using UHU or a similar glue and then hand stitch as shown by the top diagram on the left or by using an embroidery stitch as shown by the bottom diagram.

Fabric fringing. This is the easiest kind of fringing to make especially when using a coarse evenly woven fabric. The first thing to do before fringing is to cut the fabric edge on the exact grain, measuring in from the edge the exact depth of fringe required and then pulling a thread exactly on that mark. Just inside this pulled thread make a line of machine stitches to hold the rest of the threads in place, before pulling out the unwanted threads very carefully one by one. If the single fringe is not thick enough back it up with another piece, hand stitching the edges together as shown in diagram 1 opposite or by machine stitching $\frac{1}{8}''$ in.

Knotted fringe as shown by diagram 2 is an applied fringe of wool, silk or any other suitable material and is made by first cutting the strands into even lengths measuring roughly three times the intended fringe depth. To do this cut a strip of card $\frac{1}{2}''$ and then pull the cut ends through the loop.

Crochet edges. Many decorative crochet stitches can be worked on the finished edges of various garments as explained on page 100. Basically the patterns are built up using a crochet hook

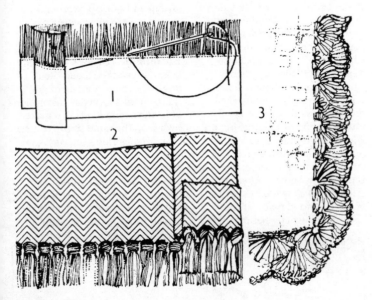

to 1″ wider than the fringe required and wrap the threads around it. Next cut along one folded edge six strands at a time. Insert a crochet hook into the finished edge and hook on the centre fold of the six strands cut. Pull the loop through the fabric which is passed through the finished edge at regular intervals, picking up a loop of working thread which when pulled through is looped many times, repeating each motif at regular intervals as shown by diagram 3 above.

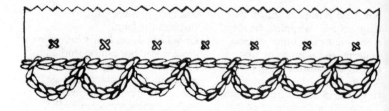

Crochet scallops. To make the crochet scallops illustrated above, first work a line of embroidered chain stitches, as explained on page 12, or a blanket stitched edge, as explained on page 10. The crochet loops are then worked through these stitches at regular intervals, passing the crochet hook through every fourth or fifth stitch, picking up a loop of working thread which is then pulled through and chain stitched to form a scallop before repeating as shown. Alternative stitches are shown on pages 100 and 101, and in many of the easy-to-follow crochet pamphlets published by the Coats Sewing Group and available through most needlework stockists or from 50 Bathwell Street, Glasgow C.2, Scotland.

Buttonhole scallops as shown below are worked along the finished edge of a garment and can be used as an edge decoration or as buttoning loops. To make each loop the same size first make four stitches along the edge over a pencil or thick knitting needle, fastening each end securely with a back stitch. Next work a blanket or buttonhole stitch over this loop as shown, fastening the thread into the turning before

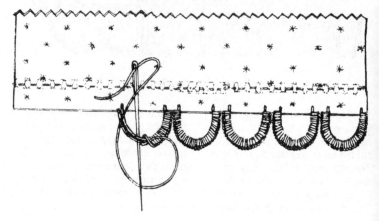

making the next loop of four threads over a pencil, etc.

Tasselled fringe. The simplest form of tasselled fringe to make is shown below, which is made out of bunches of coloured wool 6″ long which have been slotted through a blanket stitched edge and then pulled tight through its own loop.

repeat along the edge at regular intervals as shown by the diagram below.

The wool used for the tassels can be matching or contrasting in colour or the colours can be mixed to give a rainbow or graduated effect as required. String, silk or raffia can also be used in place of wool.

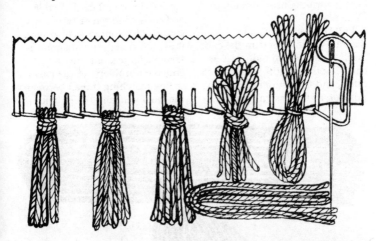

1. Work an even line of blanket stitches along the edge to be fringed.
2. Cut some coloured wool into 8″ to 10″ lengths using the card method of cutting explained on page 91, using six to eight strands at a time.
3. With the aid of a large crochet hook bring the centre fold of the wool strands through a loop in the blanket stitch and then pass the cut ends through the loop.
4. Pull the tassel tight and then

These fringes can be used on the hems and edges of bedspreads and cushions, on children's clothes or on tweed skirts as well as on nursery hangings or rag dolls. In fact they can be used in any way you choose providing they look attractive and enhance rather than detract from the total finished look.

Also try combining these edge finishes with the tassels and pom-poms explained on pages 94 to 97.

Simple Tassels. To make a simple tassel first wind some oddments of coloured wool around a strip of stiff card which is 6″ wide. Next cut along one folded edge removing six or eight strands of wool as in diagram 1.

Fold the top loop over and through itself as shown by diagram 2, making sure that the knot is forming near to the top fold.

Pull the knot tight as in diagram 3 and then trim the ends level. Make several more tassels, checking the lengths against each other, and then stitch them into position as the design requires.

As for tasselled fringes explained on page 93, the wool used can be matching or contrasting in colour, or the colours used can be mixed or alternated to give a rainbow or graduated effect as required. Alternatively string, silk or raffia can be used in place of wool.

To make a thicker tassel first cut a strip of stiff card 4″ wide and then wind ten or twelve strands of coloured wool around it as shown opposite, diagram 1. Using a large-eyed round-ended embroidery needle pass a strong matching thread between the wool and card, looping it

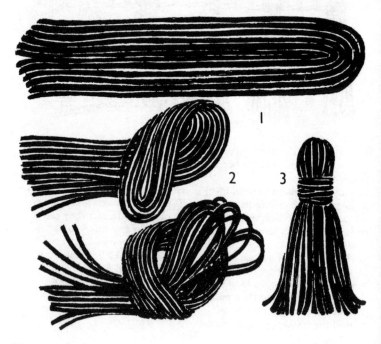

94

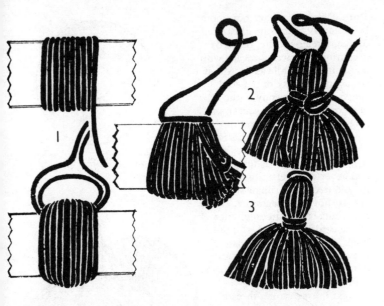

round twice as shown by diagram 2, knotting it securely. Using a sharp pair of scissors cut the wool along the bottom edge.

At $\frac{1}{2}''$ to $1''$ down from the top fold wind a strand of wool around the tassel to form a collar, knotting the ends together securely and then slotting them through the tassel with the darning needle before cutting them neatly as in diagram 3.

Make several tassels, varying the colours and textures as needed before sewing them into position with the top knotted thread.

Ornate Tassels can be made out of fancy braids and ribbons in much the same way as making the simple tassels explained opposite.

Following the illustrations above first cut a strip of card 4" wide and then wind a yard of coloured russia braid or thin ribbon around it.

Next slot a strip of braid along the top of the card under the russia braid, looping it around twice as shown in diagram 2 before knotting it securely. Using a sharp pair of scissors cut along the opposite edge and then remove the card.

About 1" down from the top fold, wind another piece of braid around the tassel to form a collar and then complete as previously explained.

Pom-Poms. To make pom-pom balls similar to the one illustrated in diagram 4 opposite, begin by preparing two circles of card with a hole in the middle as shown on the right. The size of the card can vary from a penny to the lid of a cocoa tin or even saucer size if required. Trace around the circle and cut out two cards for each pom-pom.

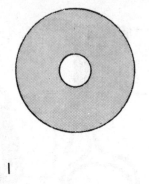

1

Place the two cards together and cover with very close stitches of coloured wool, silk or string, etc. as shown in diagram 2. When the whole of the circumference of the cards is covered, slip the point of a sharp pair of scissors between the two cards on the outer edge and cut all the threads right round the outside.

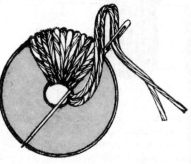

2

Next draw a strong thread through between the two cards and wind it several times very tightly around the middle threads as shown in diagram 3, fastening it off with a knot, leaving the ends as a hanging cord.

Finally, cut the card from the outer edge to the centre, taking care not to cut any of the threads, and then pull the cards out leaving the finished pom-pom as in diagram 4 opposite. Make several more pom-pom balls in matching or contrasting colours and fasten them into position by their hanging cords.

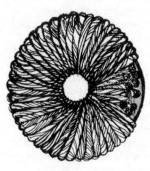

Knotted balls can be used in a similar way to pom-pom balls explained above, as bedspread

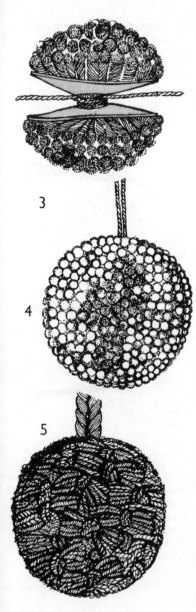

3

4

5

edgings, window blind pulls, on children's knitted hats and as scarf ends, etc., varying the colours and textures as chosen.

To make the knotted ball pom-pom as shown in diagram 5, first cut six or eight strands of wool about 3″ long. Group these together and tie a single knot in the middle, pulling the knot as tight as possible. Make a number of these knotted wool 'beads' which are then ready for attaching to the hanging cord.

To make the hanging cord cut three 12″ to 16″ lengths of wool and group these together. Fold in half and then plait together, knotting the ends as for the knotted beads, so that there is about $\frac{1}{2}$″ to $\frac{3}{4}$″ of fringed tufting below the knot. Using matching coloured strong thread, sew the fringed beads around the hanging cord knot, attaching two or three at a time and stab stitching through until finished, as in diagram 5.

The wool used for these knotted balls or the pom-poms explained opposite can be matching or contrasting in colour, or the colours can be mixed to give a graduated or rainbow look, changing the effect as required. **Simple crochet.** This interesting method of making lacey fabrics by the simple use of a crochet hook and thread may seem a little complicated at first glance, but the stitches are surprisingly simple to work. The first thing is to purchase the correct crochet hook for the chosen thread—here a Milward needlework stockist will be able to advise, for the threads can vary from the readily obtainable Mercer crochet threads available in a wide range of colours to dyed

forefinger, pulling the loop closed around the crochet hook.

2. Pass the hook under the thread and catch the thread with the hook—'threading over'. Draw thread through the loop on hook making one ch.st. Repeat until you have as many sts. as you

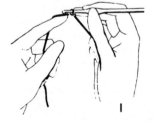

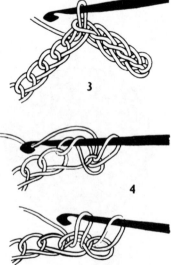

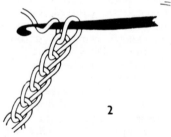

string, braid, raffia, ribbons, coloured wools, etc.

Chain Stitch (ch.st.). Make a simple loop at the end of the thread through which the crochet needle can be passed.

1. Loop the thread round the little finger of the left hand, across the palm and behind the

need, remembering that one loop must always remain on the hook and that your left thumb and forefinger should be kept near to the stitch on which you are working.

3. **Slip stitch (s.st.).** Having made between 20 and 30 ch.sts. work back along the chain with

s.sts. by inserting the hook from the front under the two top threads of each ch.st. to the left of the hook, catching thread with the hook, threading over, and drawing through, keeping the new loop on hook. Repeat ch.sts. as required.

4. **Double crochet (d.c.)**
Insert hook from the front under the two top threads of second ch.st. from hook, catch thread and draw thread through so that you have two loops on the hook. Thread over and draw through the two loops so that only one loop is left on hook, making one d.c.st. as in diagram 5.

6. **Treble crochet (tr)** is similar to double crochet but is worked with three loops on the hook instead of two. Pass the hook under the thread as shown, thread over, and pull through so that three loops are on the hook, thread over and pull through so that two loops are on the hook as in diagram 7. Thread over again and pull through the remaining two loops, one loop remaining on hook as in diagram 8.

The stitches illustrated are only a few of the numerous stitches which can be used in crochet. Many more decorative stitches can be easily learnt from the easy-to-follow crochet pamphlets published by the Coats Sewing Group and available at most Milward/Mercer needlework stockists or direct from 50 Bothwell Street, Glasgow, C.2, Scotland.

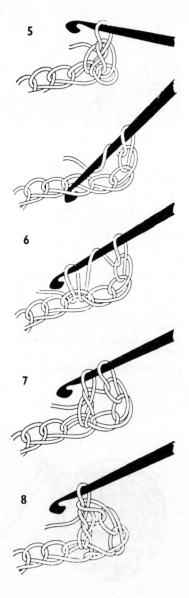

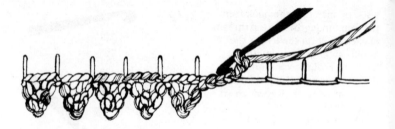

Crocheted bobbles similar to those shown below can be made by most inexperienced crocheters as they are quickly made by making a simple circle of three chain stitches and then working five slip stitches around these, then eight around the five, twelve around the eight, etc. increasing to make half the bobble and then decreasing each row to make the bobble complete. They are then filled with some cotton wool, or wool cuttings, to pad them into full bobbles.

These crochet bobbles or pom-poms can be used singly and in groups, or they can be combined with the knotted or tufted pom-poms explained on pages 96 and 97 and used as bedspread edge decoration, on children's knitted hats and tie bells, or as scarf ends, etc.

Crocheted twirls as shown by the bottom illustration on the right can be made in much the same way as explained for crochet bobbles, but instead of crocheting in ever increasing circles the stitches are worked in spiral fashion to form twirls.

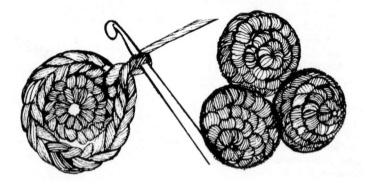

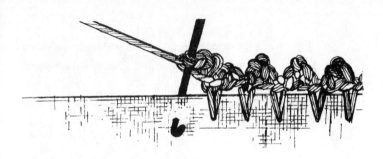

These twirls can be combined with the tassels explained on pages 94 and 95 or they can be used singly or in groups on bedspread edges, cushions, etc.

Crochet edging can be made in many different designs ranging from the finest almost lace-like edging made in silk or cotton for evening wear to the boldest chunky wool edging used on winter bedspreads. These edgings can be made as separate strips which are then sewn into position in much the same way as ready made 'shop fringes' explained on page 90, or they can be worked on to an edge as shown by the two diagrams above and on the opposite page. Basically the crochet edging is made up of stitches which are made through the finished edge, or through a row of blanket stitching which has been worked alone the edge, picking up a loop of working thread which, when pulled through, is looped many times into a motif, and then repeating the through stitch and motif looping at regular intervals until the crochet is completed.

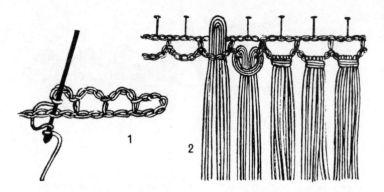

1

2

Simple fringe. To make a simple fringed edging as shown by diagrams 2 and 3, you will require a ball of soft string, knitting wool or something similar. Also a small amount of matching coloured crochet thread and a suitable crochet hook.

1. Make a simple crochet looped chain, as shown by diagram 1 above, and then pin this to the side of a cardboard box so that the loops are facing downwards.

2. Cut some 8″ to 10″ lengths of string or wool by winding them

around a 4″ or 5″ strip of firm cardboard and then cutting along one of the folded edges.

Slot five or six of the folded edges through each loop and then slot the strand ends through the folded edges before pulling tight.

3. If you would like a knotted fringe as shown by diagram 3 below, then the strand lengths should be cut 12″ to 18″ deep by winding them around a 6″ or 9″ strip of firm cardboard.

4. Next take a bunch of hanging threads, half from the left and

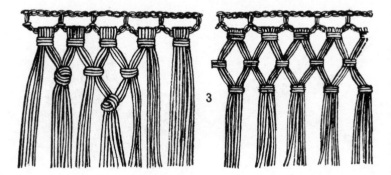

3

half from the right, and knot them together, repeating with half from the left and half from the right all the way along the row to form the top row of knots.

5. To make the second row of knots, again divide the bunches of threads which hang from each knot, taking half from the left and half from the right and knotting together so that the new knots come between those of the row above.

6. To attach this simple fringing, or a similar ready-made one, first surface-pin it into position 2 and then stab-stitch along the crocheted edge with matching coloured cotton.

Knotted fringe. The simplest knotted fringe to make is explained above and illustrated by diagram 3 opposite. However, if you wish to be more adventurous, instead of knotting groups of threads together, single threads are knotted, twisted and looped as shown by the diagrams top right, which when finished can look as decorative as the macramé work shown on the right. This knotted string macramé work can also be made into long lengths for belts and insets as well as for curtain edges or bedspreads, etc. Beads can also be used, threading them into position in between the groups of knots, as can dried seeds, small corks, pieces of plastic tubing or anything else that makes an interesting pattern and textured design.

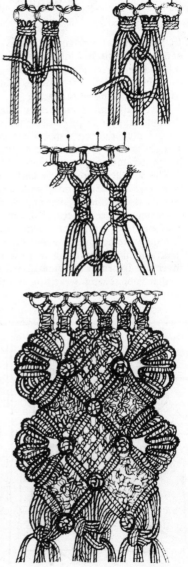

5. Sewing & Trimmings

In the previous four chapters we have explained many different kinds of decorative stitches and applied decorations. To complete the book this chapter on sewing and trimmings is intended to explain some of the other decorative techniques which are more usually associated with dressmaking and tailoring.

First of all some thought must be given to your sewing equipment, the most important piece being a sewing machine. Now it need not be an automatic, super-special one covered in gadgets. An ordinary straightforward upright straight-stitch machine, not necessarily new but preferably at least reconditioned is quite adequate.

The next items are an iron and ironing board—the normal household ones are ideal—and a work table. Small items like 6″ scissors, tape measure, thimble, pins and needles—preferably new, but never rusty ones—dressmakers' chalk, and a ruler, should all be kept in a cardboard box with your sewing threads and useful bits and pieces.

Finally, remember to avoid fussing endlessly over your sewing, hand stitching everything as if the sewing machine had never been invented. Instead work quietly and cleanly, simplifying every detail so that your sewing is exciting and full of fun.

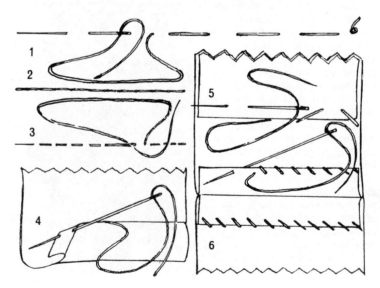

1. **Tacking.** Long even hand-stitches used for marking or for attaching pieces of fabric together for machining, fitting, etc.

2. **Machining.** A continuous stitch made by a sewing machine for joining fabrics together and for holding edges flat.

3. **Running stitch.** A small hand stitch made by passing the needle in and out of the fabric making several stitches at once.

4. **Slip stitch.** A stitch which is worked between two layers of fabric in such a way as to conceal them from the front.

5. **Catch stitch** is used to hold interlinings into position by catching alternately the fitting line and the interlining.

6. **Overcasting.** A slanting stitch used on raw edges to prevent them from unravelling as shown in diagram 6.

7. **Flat seam.** Place the fabric pieces face to face and edge to edge, matching stitching along the fitting lines before pressing open and neatening the raw edges.

8. **French seam.** A self-neatening seam made by using two lines of machining, concealing the turnings in the fold.

9. **Machined hem.** The simplest of all hems to make. First fold a scant $\frac{1}{4}''$ and then a second $\frac{1}{4}''$ or up to $1''$ before machine stitching as in 9 or 10.

11. **Embroidered hem.** Many embroidery stitches can be used to neaten hems in addition to the French knot shown in diagram 11, as explained on pages 83 to 87, etc.

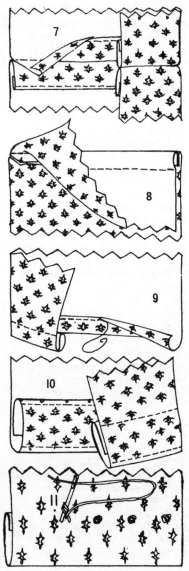

1. **Spot tacking.** This is a double stitch made in double tacking cotton through double material, with a loop left as shown on the right, so that when the pattern is removed and the fabric is pulled apart the threads are snipped between so that an identical tufted marking stitch is left on each piece.

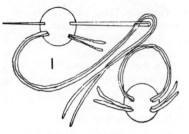

2. **Buttonholes** can be made automatically on most modern sewing machines, or they can be hand-stitched as shown on the right or using a close blanket stitch as on page 10.

First mark the buttonhole accurately with the length being on the exact grain, the size being $\frac{1}{8}''$ larger than the button and beginning on the centre front line, generally about $\frac{1}{2}''$ to $\frac{3}{4}''$ away from the edge.

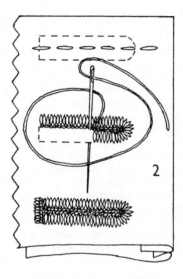

Next machine or hand run-stitch around the buttonhole $\frac{1}{8}''$ away from the centre tacking, forming a round in the front as shown. Cut along the middle and then oversew the raw edges to prevent fraying if required.

Working from right to left work purl edge buttonhole stitch as shown, or work from left to right using the blanket stitch shown on page 10, making the stitches $\frac{1}{8}''$ deep and every $\frac{1}{16}''$ to $\frac{1}{8}''$ depending on the fabric.

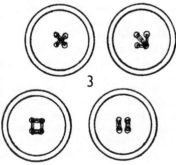

To make the round corner work six small over-stitches around to the other side, finishing the buttonhole with an end bar worked over several strands of thread, or use a bullion stitch.

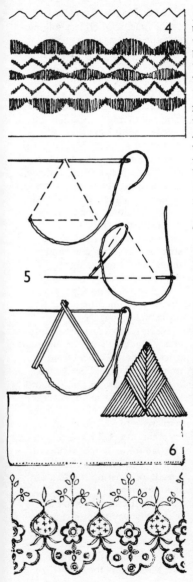

3. **Buttons** should be sewn on to their exact position, preferably with a shank which allows the button to move freely over the buttonhole without straining. When attaching leave $\frac{1}{8}''$ to $\frac{1}{4}''$ between the button and the fabric, twisting the thread around these strands to form the shank.

4. **Machine embroidery,** as with hand embroidery, can be used to decorate many garments. Usually a wide range of easy-to-make stitches are available on most modern sewing machines ranging from zig-zag shirring for children's smocks to colourful cord-work for evening skirts.

5. **Arrow heads.** These can be be used both decoratively or to add strength at the top of a pleat or end of a pocket. First mark a $\frac{1}{2}''$ to $\frac{3}{4}''$ triangle with chalk or tacking. Make the first stitch from the lower left corner taking the needle up to the top and bringing it through $\frac{1}{16}''$ to the left as shown. Next take the needle to the bottom right passing the stitch underneath and out $\frac{1}{16}''$ before the first stitch. Continue in this way, laying each thread inside the previous one, gradually filling the triangle to complete the arrowhead.

6. **Lace edging.** The simplest method of applying lace edge on to a finished garment is to lap the edge $\frac{1}{4}''$ over the lace edge and machine stitch through both thicknesses $\frac{1}{8}''$ away from the edge. An alternative method is explained overleaf.

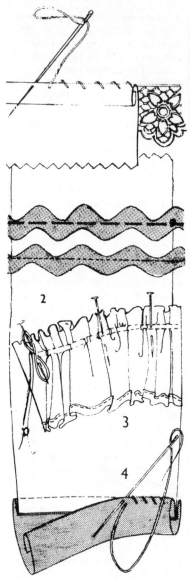

1. **Lace Edging.** An alternative to the machined on lace edging explained on page 107 is by hand-stitching as in diagram 1 on the left.

To attach the lace strip by hand place the right side of the lace against the right side of the fabric with edges together and oversew as shown.

2. **Set-ons.** Many braids, cords and ribbons can be set on top of a fabric by first tacking and then top-stitching them into position as shown by the rick-rack braid on the left and on page 50, etc.

3. **Gathered frill.** Cut a crossway or straight-grained strip of fabric twice to three times the finished length required. Double turn in and neaten the outside edge with a simple machined hem as explained on page 105.

Next, using a larger, slightly looser machine stitch, make two rows $\frac{1}{8}''$ apart $\frac{1}{4}''$ away from the unneatened edge. Tie the four threads together at one end and tie the two top threads together at the other end. Now tie the remaining two bottom threads together and pull these to gather the frill to the length required before re-knotting to hold the length, or twisting round a pin as in diagram 3.

4. **Bound edge.** Prepare a $1''$ wide crossway strip in the manner explained on page 118. Lay this strip face to face on the edge to be bound and stitch the two thicknesses together $\frac{1}{4}''$ in

from the raw edges.

Turn strip over the raw edges and turn in a $\frac{1}{4}''$ of the binding before hand stitching into position along the back of the machine line. Alternatively tack the binding edges into position and machine stitch $\frac{1}{8}''$ away from the fold as explained on page 120.

5. **Ribbon frilling.** Many ready-made ribbons or lace edgings have a special gathering thread woven along the centre or inside edges that will gather and frill the ribbon. Simply pull this thread for the effect required and then machine stitch into position. Ordinary ribbon can also be used in the same way by first making a largish slightly loose machine gathering stitch in matching thread as explained for a gathered frill opposite, or use a special machine gathering attachment which automatically gathers 3 to 1. Also turn to page 42 for other ideas.

6. **Inset Edges.** This method of attaching decorative trimmings has the advantage of enclosing all the raw edges inside a facing strip, and is particularly suitable for curved or scalloped edges. The trimmings used can be ribbons, braid, rick-rack, lace, broderie anglaise, rouleaux strips or frills. For the illustration on the right folded ribbon was used.

First tack the folded ribbon or other edging into position, right sides together. Cover with a machine-neatened facing strip and then stitch through all

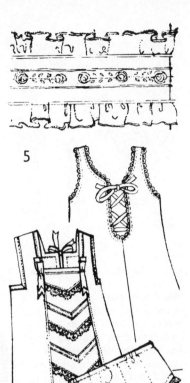

5

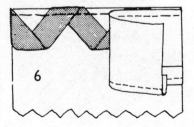

6

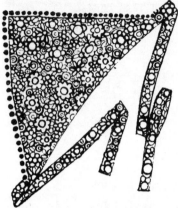

fancy-knit winter stockings.
Team these with gloves,
berets, scarves or even a rose-
embroidered sweater and
cardigan for a co-ordinated look.
Some of the stitches used for
this type of embroidery are
explained in Chapter 1, with
many more being easily learned
from the numerous pamphlets
and transfer designs on sale at
most sewing shops. As well as the
great variety of stitches, there are

thicknesses $\frac{1}{8}''$ or $\frac{1}{4}''$ from the raw
edges. Turn facing to wrong
side and neaten as for a normal
hem.

Wool Embroidery can be very
attractive when used in different
ways on all sorts of ready-made
garments, such as adding some
wool roses or lazy daisies as
explained on page 14 on to a pair
of children's knee socks or

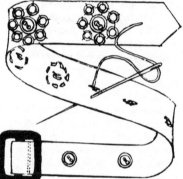

also a great variety of threads
which can be used in addition to
coloured wools, including string,
russia braid, ribbons, strips of
leather and plastic, beads and
many, many novelties.

Decorative belts. Many
different belts can be made by
plaiting coloured ribbons together,
knotting string, and adding
beads, or by couching, cording
and appliquéing, etc., or by
decorating a ready-made webbing
belt with a pattern of odd buttons,
brass curtain rings, metal loops
and other decorative oddments.

Collect together as many beads, old metal, bone or pearl buttons as you can find, arranging and stitching them on as explained on page 39.

Decorative buttons can generally be purchased in most department stores in a wide variety of sizes and interesting designs, ranging from shaped seeds and plastic pieces. Simply try several out as explained on page 38, experimenting until you have made several to choose from, changing the designs until they are right.

Tuck making. This is a very traditional form of decorating a surface that relies not only on interesting groupings or gradua-

metal, coloured cordings, moulded glass and plastic to jewelled and sequinned buttons. Similarly, decorative buckles are also available, or button and buckle sets can easily be made by twisting, looping, twirling, plaiting or knotting cord, raffia, rouleaux, dyed string, pipe cleaners, or even electrical wire covering, and incorporating beads, sequins, motifs, dried

tions of tucks, but also on the accuracy of spacing and stitching in order to enhance rather than detract from the finished look. Each tuck should be made on the exact grain, creasing along the grain line to mark the position accurately before stitching, measuring between each tuck with a notched cardboard guide.

As it is almost impossible to judge exactly how much extra

material is required for a particular tucked area it is wisest to cut the material much larger than the pattern, tucking as required before trimming accurately to shape.

Pin tucks. These are very narrow tucks which can be arranged in groups or evenly spaced. They can be made automatically on many of the modern twin-needle sewing

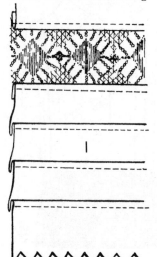

machines, which can also raise and cord them, or they can be made on most other sewing machines by accurately top stitching $\frac{1}{8}''$ away from a folded edge of fabric. As explained overleaf, accuracy of marking is essential, as each tuck must be on the exact grain, creasing along to mark neatly before stitching close to the folded edge, using a notched guide to space each tuck accurately.

Wide tucks are made in a similar way to pin tucks, but instead of stitching $\frac{1}{8}''$ away from the creased edge the stitching is usually $\frac{1}{4}''$ to $\frac{1}{2}''$ in. When measuring the distances between each tuck an extra allowance of between $\frac{1}{2}''$ to $1''$ must be made to allow for the tuck under lap. So experiment with various

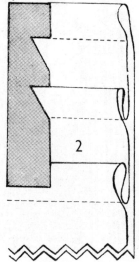

depths and distances, cutting a double notched guide below before tucking the actual area required.

Tuck guide. Cut a $4''$ by $1''$ strip of stiff cardboard, squaring the corners accurately. Measure $\frac{1}{2}''$, or width of tuck required, away from the top and make a $\frac{1}{4}''$ cut parallel to the top, making a second cut diagonally from below the first to make a triangular

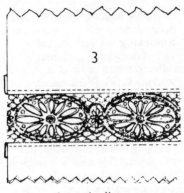

3

machine carefully, experimenting on odd strips of fabric before making the tucked area required.

Tuck insets as shown in diagrams 1 and 3 can be used in between groups of tucks, or separately as required. The insets are made by first cutting the fabric into strips, turning under $\frac{1}{4}''$ and laying the folded edge on to the lace inset, then top stitching through both thicknesses $\frac{1}{8}''$ away from the folded edge. Repeat on other side,

notch, as shown in diagram 2 on the left. Make a second straight cut 1″ away from the first, or distance required between tuck and stitching, again notching out a diagonal.

Air tucks. Many twin-needle machines make automatic tucks which can also be raised and corded. As the exact working instructions differ between the various makes, follow the instructions supplied with the

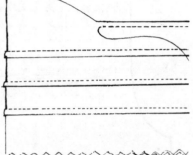

tucking and insetting to complete the area as needed.

Cross tucks are a variation of normal pin or air tucks, and when arranged in groups they give a very attractive look. This type of tucking across tucks is ideal for collars and cuffs, tabs and pockets, on children's clothes or evening separates, etc. As with the other tucks already explained, accuracy of marking and neatness of stitching is essential, as the idea is to enhance rather than detract from the finished look of a garment.

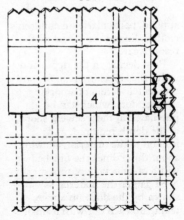

4

Shirring or decorative gathering may be made either by hand or by machine, and is used to gather in fullness evenly. In order to ensure even spacing for the gathering stitches, measure the gaps with a notched guide as for pin tucks, explained on page 112.

For hand shirring used in small areas of smocking, make an even running stitch along the marked lines, leaving a reason-

costumes, lingerie, casual summer dresses, etc.

Smocking is a very attractive way of decorating gathered fullness, which consists of working various ornamental stitches into geometric groups on top of the small tucks formed by the even gathering. The use of smocking varies with the changing moods of fashion, but as a general rule wherever fullness is shown smocking may be

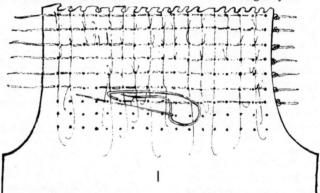

able length of thread at each end for pulling up, adjusting the fullness evenly before fastening the threads securely.

Machine shirring is usually made with a special elasticated shirring thread wound on to the machine spool. The stitch length and tension should be adjusted as detailed on the shirring elastic information sheet, and then tested on odd lengths before stitching the actual area required. Elasticated shirring can be used on children's wear, swimming

applied, particularly on children's clothes, lingerie or casual and resort wear.

First decide on the depth and width the smocking is to be, and then cut a section of smocking transfer dots, which can be purchased at most sewing shops, to the depth required, and iron on to the material, allowing about three times the finished width of smocking required. Next gather the material as shown by the diagram above, taking up each dot with a small stitch evenly across the fabric, securing the thread at the beginning of each row with a knot and leaving ample threads at the other end for pulling-up. When all the rows have been worked, draw up the threads sufficiently tight to allow the pleats to be stroked into place with a pin so that they lay evenly and can be easily smocked, securing the ends around a pin as for a gathered frill, explained on page 108.

Finally, work the smocking stitches to make a decorative pattern before removing the gathering stitches.

Cable smocking. Working from left to right over a line of dots on top of regularly gathered pleats, bring the thread up through the first dot, picking up next dot with thread above the needle and draw up. Pick up third dot with thread below the needle as in diagram A on the right. Repeat the cable stitch with the thread alternating above and below the needle right along the line.

Honeycomb. Working from left to right over alternate lines of dots on top of regularly gathered pleats, bring the needle out of the first dot on lower line. With the thread below the needle pick up the next dot—number 1 in the diagram—draw-stitch together, next pick up dot above last dot—number 2 on the diagram—with thread above the needle pick up next dot—number 3 on the diagram—and draw-

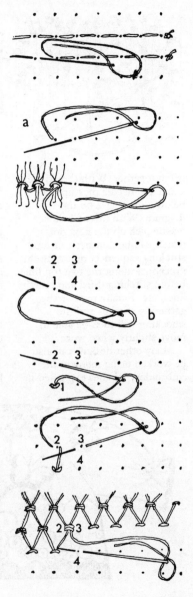

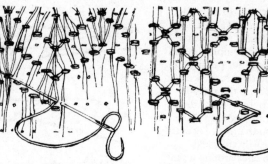

stitch together. With thread still above the needle pick up dot below—number 4 on the diagram. With thread below needle pick up the next dot which will be number 1 of next stitching sequence, repeating this procedure along the two top lines before stitching third and fourth lines, etc. Finally remove the gathering stitches and the smocking will then be able to move slightly when worn.

Many other designs can also be worked using many of the embroidery stitches explained in chapter 1, as shown by the zig-zag and diamond patterns illustrated above worked in simple stem stitch, explained on page 9.

The zig-zag pattern is worked in lines $\frac{1}{2}''$ apart, each line being made by making five stitches up and then five stitches down, each stitch taking up one pleat.

The diamond pattern is made by working four stitches up and then four stitches down, each stitch taking up one pleat. The second row, which forms the lower half of the diamond, is

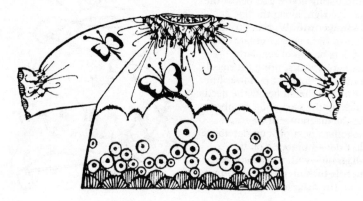

worked so that the upper point of the group of stitches will touch the lower ones of the previous group.

Rouleaux Trimmings. The use of bias rouleaux tubing as trimmings in dressmaking is coming back into fashion for use as looped buttonholes and froggings, for belts and bows, as insets and set-ons, or for

To make the bias tubing, fold the cut bias strip to half its width with the right side inside, and stitch $\frac{1}{8}''$ from the edge, keeping the stitching an even distance from the edge. For turning the tubing right side out, insert a flat bodkin or tapestry needle in one end, and with a fine sewing needle and thread sew the material to the eye of the bodkin.

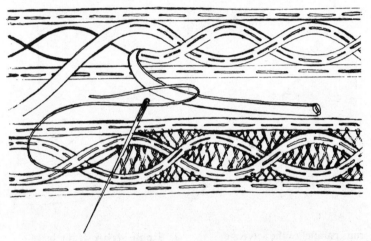

piping and edgings, the variety of effects possible being quite unlimited.

The tubing consists of bias strips of material, cut as explained on page 118, which have been sewn to form tubes varying from $\frac{1}{8}''$ to $\frac{3}{8}''$, depending on the type of material used. For the narrowest tubing, using fine crepe or lawn, cut bias strips $\frac{1}{2}''$ wide; the wider tubings of thicker fabric require bias strips $1''$ wide.

Now push the bodkin through the tube, turning the fabric right side out.

If a soft cord-like effect is required, leave the tubing unpressed, but if it is to be used as looped buttonholes or froggings as shown on pages 122 to 124, or as a decorative inset as shown above, press the tubing, curving it to shape as you press, with the stitched edge on the underside of the curve.

117

1. **Bias strip.** To make the bias strip used for the rouleaux trimmings explained on page 117, or as a binding as on page 120, fold the fabric as in diagram 1. The true bias grain or crossway runs diagonally across the fabric. This diagonal line can be found by folding the corner of the fabric over so that the cut end

3. **Continuous strip.** Fold the marked strip into a tube so that the ends are placed one mark up as shown below, with the lines forming a continuous spiral, right side of fabric inside. Stitch the seam together and press open. Cut into a continuous strip along the spiralling lines, restitching each separate seam for strength.

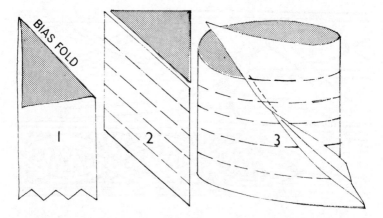

runs parallel to the selvedge edge. Crease along the fold and then cut along the crease line.
2. **Cutting bias.** Chalk-mark on the wrong side of the fabric several parallel lines the required distances away from the bias cut edge, as shown in diagram 2 above, cutting along the last line only, the distance between each line being $\frac{5}{8}''$ for a narrow bias piping or $1''$ or more for a wider one, or up to $3''$ or $4''$ if the strip is being used decoratively.

4. **Single strips.** If the bias strip is being made from several individually cut crossway pieces of fabric, then these should be joined along their straight grains, giving a short diagonal seam as shown in diagram 4 on the right. Press each seam open to obtain a continuous strip.
5. **Corded piping** is used on edges and seams in both dress-making and in household sewing. To make a corded piping cut a length of piping cord $1''$ longer

than the length required and place it on to the wrong side of the prepared bias strip. Fold the strip in half so that the raw edges meet and tack stitch through the turnings so that the cord is pushed tightly against the folded edge of the binding. Using a piping foot attachment on the sewing machine, stitch close to the cord over the top of the tacking.

6. **Joining piping.** Cut along the exact grain lines of the two piping pieces to be joined so that they are complementing diagonals. Cut the righthand cord $\frac{1}{2}''$ short and fold under a $\frac{1}{4}''$ turning, leaving the other cord protruding $\frac{1}{4}''$ as in diagram 6. Slot ends together so that the fold covers the raw edges and slip-stitch together.

7. **Piped seams.** Lay the prepared piping on to the seam so that the raw edges are together and the piping stitched line exactly matches the fitting lines. Tack piping into position before stitching together as for normal insets, explained on page 109, using a piping foot attachment to get close to the cord so that stitching goes over the top of the tacking. If there is a square corner, snip the piping turnings as shown in diagram 7.

8. **Curved piping.** If a curved seam is to be piped then the turnings of the piping will need to be notched at $\frac{1}{4}''$ intervals as shown on the right. The piping is then attached in the normal way.

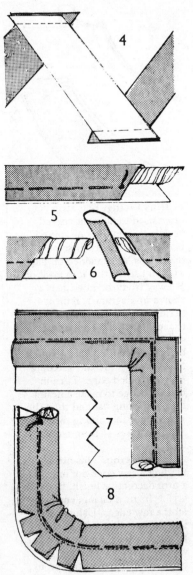

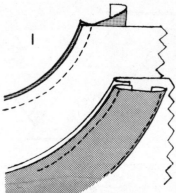

the edge, right sides together, and stitch to the required width. Trim strip turnings to $\frac{1}{8}''$ before turning binding to the wrong side, turning in the raw edge and hand-stitching into position along the back of the machine stitching as shown in diagram 2 below.

Extra care should be taken on all curved edges, easing the binding on around the corners so that it does not twist or pucker. An alternative method

1. **Bias facing.** Bias strip is often used to face out curved necklines, armholes or curved pockets, etc. First cut some $1''$ bias strips, as explained on page 118, and stitch this into position $\frac{1}{4}''$ away from the raw edges as shown in diagram 1, remembering to place the fabrics face to face. Next clip the curved seam to $\frac{1}{8}''$ and snip in every $\frac{1}{4}''$ before turning the bias strip on to the wrong side and stitching $\frac{1}{8}''$ from folded edge. Turn in bias raw edge to make a neat $\frac{1}{2}''$ facing, tacking flat and then slip stitching or machining through all thicknesses $\frac{1}{8}''$ from tacked fold.

2. **Bias edging.** This method of binding a raw edge not only gives a firm decorative finish, but also acts as its own facing, enclosing all the raw edges. Using a bias strip of matching or contrasting fabric, cut four times the finished width—just over $1''$ for a $\frac{1}{4}''$ binding—place this strip on to

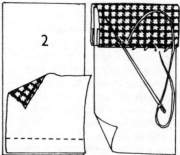

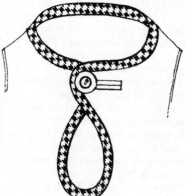

of binding which is usually made with ready-made bias strip or similarly prepared fabric strip is to attach the binding by machine. First cut the strip 1¼″ wide and next fold in a scant ¼″ along both edges, then fold in half along the entire length and press along the centre fold. Place this folded tube over the fabric edge and tack, then machine into position over the tacking through all thicknesses.

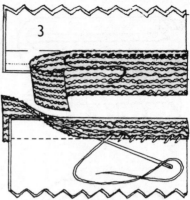

3. **Braiding,** like binding, is a very decorative and useful edge neatening. Braids can be bought by the yard in many colours in silk or wool textures. First mark the edge the depth of braiding required and then tack the braiding to this mark, right side uppermost, tacking then machining into position as in diagram 3. Turn braid to the wrong side and hand-stitch on to the back of the machine line.

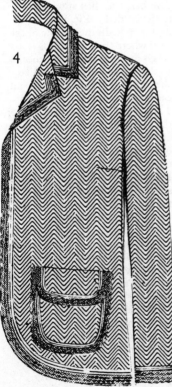

Russia braid is another decorative form of braiding generally used to outline interesting design details in the same way as top-stitching. This thin twin-corded braid is attached by either machine-stitching along the centre fold, or by neatly stab-stitching every ¼″ as for Soutache braiding on page 88. The jacket on the left has wool braid over its raw edges with a russia braid inset.

Corded rouleaux. To make a corded rouleaux for a tie belt or loop buttoning, first cut the

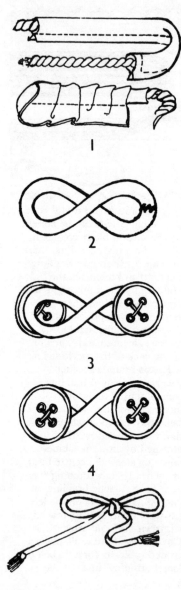

1

2

3

4

fabric on the bias grain as explained on page 118, making the width sufficient to go round the chosen cord plus turnings— a $\frac{1}{4}''$ cord requiring a $1''$ to $1\frac{1}{4}''$ bias strip. Cut the fabric the length required but cut the cord twice that length—the extra length being required to make the stitching easier and for aiding the turning through.

Fold the right side of the fabric over the first half of the cord, tacking the fabric edges together, and then stitch close to the corded fabric, using a piping foot. In the middle of the cord where the fabric ends stitch through all the thicknesses so that when the cord is pulled the rouleaux turns right side out, easing the fabric over the cord a little at a time. Cut to $1''$ longer than required, snipping away $\frac{3}{4}''$ of cord at each end, turn in $\frac{1}{2}''$ of fabric and slip stitch ends together.

Rouleaux tabs. Many variations and designs can be made by twisting, plaiting or looping the rouleaux tube to form tab type buttoning, the simplest of which are shown on the left, whilst the more complicated designs— known as froggings—are shown by diagram 6 opposite and on page 124.

To make the simplest looped tab fastening cut an $8''$ length of $\frac{1}{4}''$ rouleaux tubing and clip away $\frac{1}{2}''$ of cord from each end. Tuck in fabric ends and slip-stitch these together as shown in diagram 2, also slip-stitching the looped crossing. Sew two 1″ buttons 2½″ apart and secure the tab join behind one of the buttons as in diagram 3, fastening and unfastening the other side as required.

Rouleaux bows can be made in much the same way as ribbon or fabric bows. A simple bow is shown by diagram 4 opposite,

long for ½″ buttons—and tack these into position at ½″ or 1″ intervals, or as required. Cover with a facing strip as for normal inset edges explained on page 109 and then stitch through all thicknesses ¼″ away from the raw edges. Turn facing through to the wrong side and stitch down in the normal way.

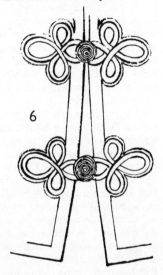

but the size and shape can vary as required. Simply try out several before deciding which is best, and then try out several more to make sure that you were right.

Rouleaux buttonholes as shown by diagram 5 below are generally made out of soft tubing as explained on page 117—that is without a centre cord. Cut the tubing into even lengths—2″

Froggings. Decorative fastenings can be made with soft or corded rouleaux strips, or ready-made fancy cord and braiding by twisting, plaiting, or looping the rouleaux or cording to many different designs in addition to the one shown in diagram 6 above.

First rough out the shape required on to a piece of stiff paper, shaping the rouleaux or

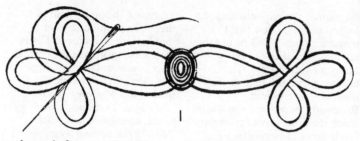

ready-made fancy cord to this shape and pin; then tack into position, with the seam uppermost. Stitch the looped crossings together securely before removing from the paper, and then neatly attach to the garment as shown in diagram 1 above.

If the ends consist of a tight twirl as in diagram 2 below, care should be taken to sew the edges together neatly as shown. The curves should be shaped and lightly pressed as needed, making sure that the stitched edges fall at the back just inside the curve so that they do not show when the fastening is complete, as in diagram 3, taking care to repeat each twirl accurately.

Rouleaux buttons can be made by twisting, looping, twirling, plaiting or knotting soft or corded rouleaux as well as using braids and decorative cords, dyed string, pipe-cleaners or even electrical wire covering. Simply try several out and if they are successful hand-stitch them together, concealing the stitches as much as possible, as explained on page 38.

Jewelled buttons and fancy cuff-links can also be made in much the same way, as can decorative buckles, beaded belts or any number of other pretty things. So when you feel like sewing try making something different for a change. Remember that your sewing should be an exciting challenge which has no inhibiting rules; it will then not only be quicker and easier to do, but will also be thoroughly enjoyable and fun as well.

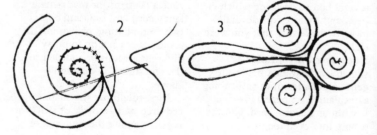

INDEX